TEST PREPARATION SERIES

W9-AFB-546

Get Ready!

FOR STANDARDIZED TESTS

READING, GRADE ONE

1

Molly Maack

Carol Turkington
Series Editor

McGraw-Hill

New York   Chicago   San Francisco
Lisbon   London   Madrid   Mexico City
Milan   New Delhi   San Juan   Seoul
Singapore   Sydney   Toronto

Library of Congress Cataloging-in-Publication Data

Get ready! for standardized tests. Reading.
    p. cm.—(Test preparation series)
    Contents:—[v. 1] Grade one / Molly Maack—[v. 2] Grade two / Louise Ulrich—[v. 3] Grade three / Joanne Baker—[v. 4] Grade four / Kris Callahan.
    ISBN 0-07-137405-1 (pbk. : v. 1)—ISBN 0-07-137406-X (pbk. : v. 2)—ISBN 0-07-137407-8 (pbk. : v. 3)—ISBN 0-07-137408-6 (pbk. : v. 4)
    1. Achievement tests—United States—Study guides.   2. Reading (Elementary)—United States—Evaluation.   3. Reading (Elementary)—Parent participation—United States.   I. Ulrich, Louise.   II. Test preparation series (McGraw-Hill Companies)

LB3060.22 .G48   2001
372.126'2—dc21   2001030896

McGraw-Hill

A Division of The McGraw·Hill Companies

1 2 3 4 5 6 7 8 9 0 COU/COU 0 9 8 7 6 5 4 3 2 1

ISBN 0-07-137405-1

This book was set in New Century Schoolbook by Inkwell Publishing Services.

Printed and bound by Courier.

McGraw-Hill books are available at special quantity discounts to use as premiums and sales promotions, or for use in corporate training programs. For more information, please write to the Director of Special Sales, McGraw-Hill, Professional Publishing, Two Penn Plaza, New York, NY 10121-2298. Or contact your local bookstore.

Get Ready!

FOR STANDARDIZED TESTS

READING, GRADE ONE

Other Books in the *Get Ready!* Series:

To my son, Watson Gregory Maack, who I look forward to teaching how to read independently and how to apply the skills in this book. I hope he will one day develop a love of reading.

Molly Maack

Contents

SKILLS CHECKLIST

MY CHILD …	HAS LEARNED	IS WORKING ON
WORD ANALYSIS		
LETTER RECOGNITION		
VOCABULARY		
SYNONYMS		
ANTONYMS		
WORD MEANINGS IN CONTEXT		
BEGINNING WORD SOUNDS		
ENDING WORD SOUNDS		
VOWEL SOUNDS		
RHYMING SOUNDS		
SPELLING		
CAPITALIZATION		
PUNCTUATION		
WORD USAGE		
READING COMPREHENSION		
LISTENING COMPREHENSION		
PICTURE COMPREHENSION		
SENTENCE COMPREHENSION		
STORY COMPREHENSION		

Introduction

Almost all of us have taken standardized tests in school. We spent several days bubbling-in answers, shifting in our seats. No one ever told us why we took the tests or what they would do with the results. We just took them and never heard about them again.

Today many parents aren't aware they are entitled to see their children's permanent records and, at a reasonable cost, to obtain copies of any information not protected by copyright, including testing scores. Late in the school year, most parents receive standardized test results with confusing bar charts and detailed explanations of scores that few people seem to understand.

In response to a series of negative reports on the state of education in this country, Americans have begun to demand that something be done to improve our schools. We have come to expect higher levels of accountability as schools face the competing pressures of rising educational expectations and declining school budgets. High-stakes standardized tests are rapidly becoming the main tool of accountability for students, teachers, and school administrators. If students' test scores don't continually rise, teachers and principals face the potential loss of school funding and, ultimately, their jobs. Summer school and private after-school tutorial program enrollments are swelling with students who have not met score standards or who, everyone agrees, could score higher.

While there is a great deal of controversy about whether it is appropriate for schools to use standardized tests to make major decisions about individual students, it appears likely that standardized tests are here to stay. They will be used to evaluate students, teachers, and the schools; schools are sure to continue to use students' test scores to demonstrate their accountability to the community.

The purposes of this guide are to acquaint you with the types of standardized tests your children may take; to help you understand the test results; and to help you work with your children in skill areas that are measured by standardized tests so they can perform as well as possible.

Types of Standardized Tests

The two major types of group standardized tests are *criterion-referenced tests* and *norm-referenced tests*. Think back to when you learned to tie your shoes. First Mom or Dad showed you how to loosen the laces on your shoe so that you could insert your foot; then they showed you how to tighten the laces—but not too tight. They showed you how to make bows and how to tie a knot. All the steps we just described constitute what is called a *skills hierarchy:* a list of skills from easiest to most difficult that are related to some goal, such as tying a shoelace.

Criterion-referenced tests are designed to determine at what level students are performing on various skills hierarchies. These tests assume that development of skills follows a sequence of steps. For example, if you were teaching shoelace tying, the skills hierarchy might appear this way:

1. Loosen laces.
2. Insert foot.
3. Tighten laces.
4. Make loops with both lace ends.
5. Tie a square knot.

Criterion-referenced tests try to identify how far along the skills hierarchy the student has progressed. There is no comparison against anyone else's score, only against an expected skill level. The main question criterion-referenced tests ask is: "Where is this child in the development of this group of skills?"

Norm-referenced tests, in contrast, are typically constructed to compare children in their abilities as to different skills areas. Although the experts who design test items may be aware of skills hierarchies, they are more concerned with how much of some skill the child has mastered, rather than at what level on the skills hierarchy the child is.

Ideally, the questions on these tests range from very easy items to those that are impossibly difficult. The essential feature of norm-referenced tests is that scores on these measures can be compared to scores of children in similar groups. They answer this question: "How does the child compare with other children of the same age or grade placement in the development of this skill?"

This book provides strategies for increasing your child's scores on both standardized norm-referenced and criterion-referenced tests.

The Major Standardized Tests

Many criterion-referenced tests currently in use are created locally or (at best) on a state level,

and there are far too many of them to go into detail here about specific tests. However, children prepare for them in basically the same way they do for norm-referenced tests.

A very small pool of norm-referenced tests is used throughout the country, consisting primarily of the Big Five:

- California Achievement Tests (CTB/McGraw-Hill)
- Iowa Tests of Basic Skills (Riverside)
- Metropolitan Achievement Test (Harcourt-Brace & Company)
- Stanford Achievement Test (Psychological Corporation)
- TerraNova [formerly Comprehensive Test of Basic Skills] (McGraw-Hill)

These tests use various terms for the academic skills areas they assess, but they generally test several types of reading, language, and mathematics skills, along with social studies and science. They may include additional assessments, such as of study and reference skills.

How States Use Standardized Tests

Despite widespread belief and practice to the contrary, group standardized tests are designed to assess and compare the achievement of groups. They are *not* designed to provide detailed diagnostic assessments of individual students. (For detailed individual assessments, children should be given individual diagnostic tests by properly qualified professionals, including trained guidance counselors, speech and language therapists, and school psychologists.) Here are examples of the types of questions group standardized tests are designed to answer:

- How did the reading achievement of students at Valley Elementary School this year compare with their reading achievement last year?

- How did math scores at Wonderland Middle School compare with those of students at Parkside Middle School this year?

- As a group, how did Hilltop High School students compare with the national averages in the achievement areas tested?

- How did the district's first graders' math scores compare with the district's fifth graders' math scores?

The fact that these tests are designed primarily to test and compare groups doesn't mean that test data on individual students isn't useful. It does mean that when we use these tests to diagnose individual students, we are using them for a purpose for which they were not designed.

Think of group standardized tests as being similar to health fairs at the local mall. Rather than check into your local hospital and spend thousands of dollars on full, individual tests for a wide range of conditions, you can go from station to station and take part in different health screenings. Of course, one would never diagnose heart disease or cancer on the basis of the screening done at the mall. At most, suspicious results on the screening would suggest that you need to visit a doctor for a more complete examination.

In the same way, group standardized tests provide a way of screening the achievement of many students quickly. Although you shouldn't diagnose learning problems solely based on the results of these tests, the results can tell you that you should think about referring a child for a more definitive, individual assessment.

An individual student's group test data should be considered only a point of information. Teachers and school administrators may use standardized test results to support or question hypotheses they have made about students; but these scores must be used alongside other information, such as teacher comments, daily work, homework, class test grades, parent observations, medical needs, and social history.

Valid Uses of Standardized Test Scores

Here are examples of appropriate uses of test scores for individual students:

- Mr. Cone thinks that Samantha, a third grader, is struggling in math. He reviews her file and finds that her first- and second-grade standardized test math scores were very low. Her first- and second-grade teachers recall episodes in which Samantha cried because she couldn't understand certain math concepts, and mention that she was teased by other children, who called her "Dummy." Mr. Cone decides to refer Samantha to the school assistance team to determine whether she should be referred for individual testing for a learning disability related to math.

- The local college wants to set up a tutoring program for elementary school children who are struggling academically. In deciding which youngsters to nominate for the program, the teachers consider the students' averages in different subjects, the degree to which students seem to be struggling, parents' reports, and standardized test scores.

- For the second year in a row, Gene has performed poorly on the latest round of standardized tests. His teachers all agree that Gene seems to have some serious learning problems. They had hoped that Gene was immature for his class and that he would do better this year; but his dismal grades continue. Gene is referred to the school assistance team to determine whether he should be sent to the school psychologist for assessment of a possible learning handicap.

Inappropriate Use of Standardized Test Scores

Here are examples of how schools have sometimes used standardized test results inappropriately:

- Mr. Johnson groups his students into reading groups solely on the basis of their standardized test scores.

- Ms. Henry recommends that Susie be held back a year because she performed poorly on the standardized tests, despite strong grades on daily assignments, homework, and class tests.

- Gerald's teacher refers him for consideration in the district's gifted program, which accepts students using a combination of intelligence test scores, achievement test scores, and teacher recommendations. Gerald's intelligence test scores were very high. Unfortunately, he had a bad cold during the week of the standardized group achievement tests and was taking powerful antihistamines, which made him feel sleepy. As a result, he scored too low on the achievement tests to qualify.

The public has come to demand increasingly high levels of accountability for public schools. We demand that schools test so that we have hard data with which to hold the schools accountable. But too often, politicians and the public place more faith in the test results than is justified. Regardless of whether it's appropriate to do so and regardless of the reasons schools use standardized test results as they do, many schools base crucial programming and eligibility decisions on scores from group standardized tests. It's to your child's advantage, then, to perform as well as possible on these tests.

Two Basic Assumptions

The strategies we present in this book come from two basic assumptions:

1. Most students can raise their standardized test scores.

2. Parents can help their children become stronger in the skills the tests assess.

This book provides the information you need

to learn what skill areas the tests measure, what general skills your child is being taught in a particular grade, how to prepare your child to take the tests, and what to do with the results. In the appendices you will find information to help you decipher test interpretations; a listing of which states currently require what tests; and additional resources to help you help your child to do better in school and to prepare for the tests.

A Word about Coaching

This guide is *not* about coaching your child. When we use the term *coaching* in referring to standardized testing, we mean trying to give someone an unfair advantage, either by revealing beforehand what exact items will be on the test or by teaching "tricks" that will supposedly allow a student to take advantage of some detail in how the tests are constructed.

Some people try to coach students in shrewd test-taking strategies that take advantage of how the tests are supposedly constructed rather than strengthening the students' skills in the areas tested. Over the years, for example, many rumors have been floated about "secret formulas" that test companies use.

This type of coaching emphasizes ways to help students obtain scores they didn't earn—to get something for nothing. Stories have appeared in the press about teachers who have coached their students on specific questions, parents who have tried to obtain advance copies of tests, and students who have written down test questions after taking standardized tests and sold them to others. Because of the importance of test security, test companies and states aggressively prosecute those who attempt to violate test security—and they should do so.

How to Raise Test Scores

Factors that are unrelated to how strong students are but that might artificially lower test scores include anything that prevents students from making scores that accurately describe their actual abilities. Some of those factors are:

- giving the tests in uncomfortably cold or hot rooms;

- allowing outside noises to interfere with test taking; and

- reproducing test booklets in such small print or with such faint ink that students can't read the questions.

Such problems require administrative attention from both the test publishers, who must make sure that they obtain their norms for the tests under the same conditions students face when they take the tests; and school administrators, who must ensure that conditions under which their students take the tests are as close as possible to those specified by the test publishers.

Individual students also face problems that can artificially lower their test scores, and parents can do something about many of these problems. Stomach aches, headaches, sleep deprivation, colds and flu, and emotional upsets due to a recent tragedy are problems that might call for the student to take the tests during make-up sessions. Some students have physical conditions such as muscle-control problems, palsies, or difficulty paying attention that require work over many months or even years before students can obtain accurate test scores on standardized tests. And, of course, some students just don't take the testing seriously or may even intentionally perform poorly. Parents can help their children overcome many of these obstacles to obtaining accurate scores.

Finally, with this book parents are able to help their children raise their scores by:

- increasing their familiarity (and their comfort level) with the types of questions on standardized tests;

- drills and practice exercises to increase their skill in handling the kinds of questions they will meet; and

- providing lots of fun ways for parents to help their children work on the skill areas that will be tested.

Test Questions

The favorite type of question for standardized tests is the multiple-choice question. For example:

1. The first President of the United States was:

   A Abraham Lincoln

   B Martin Luther King, Jr.

   C George Washington

   D Thomas Jefferson

The main advantage of multiple-choice questions is that it is easy to score them quickly and accurately. They lend themselves to optical scanning test forms, on which students fill in bubbles or squares and the forms are scored by machine. Increasingly, companies are moving from paper-based testing to computer-based testing, using multiple-choice questions.

The main disadvantage of multiple-choice questions is that they restrict test items to those that can be put in that form. Many educators and civil rights advocates have noted that the multiple-choice format only reveals a superficial understanding of the subject. It's not possible with multiple-choice questions to test a student's ability to construct a detailed, logical argument on some issue or to explain a detailed process. Although some of the major tests are beginning to incorporate more subjectively scored items, such as short answer or essay questions, the vast majority of test items continue to be in multiple-choice format.

In the past, some people believed there were special formulas or tricks to help test-takers determine which multiple-choice answer was the correct one. There may have been some truth to *some* claims for past tests. Computer analyses of some past tests revealed certain biases in how tests were constructed. For example, the old advice to pick *D* when in doubt appears to have been valid for some past tests. However, test publishers have become so sophisticated in their ability to detect patterns of bias in the formulation of test questions and answers that they now guard against it aggressively.

In Chapter 1, we provide information about general test-taking considerations, with advice on how parents can help students overcome testing obstacles. The rest of the book provides information to help parents help their children strengthen skills in the tested areas.

Joseph Harris, Ph.D.

Test-Taking Basics

You can be sure that at some time during the 12 years that your child spends in school, he will face a standardized testing situation. Some schools test every year, while others test every other year. How well your child performs on such a test can be related to many things: Did he get plenty of rest the night before? Is he anxious in testing situations? Did he get confused when filling in the answer sheets and make a mechanical mistake?

That's why educators emphasize that a child's score on a standardized test shouldn't be used as the sole criterion for evaluating how a child is learning and developing. Instead, test scores should be considered as one part of an educational picture together with the child's classroom performance and overall areas of strength and weakness. Your child won't pass or fail a standardized test, but you can often see a general pattern of strengths and weaknesses.

What This Book Can Do

This book is not designed to help your child artificially inflate his scores on a standardized test. Instead, its purpose is to help you understand the typical kinds of skills taught in a first-grade class and what a typical first grader can be expected to know by the end of the year. It also presents lots of fun activities that you can use at home to work with your child in particular skill areas that may be weak. This book is not meant to replace your child's teacher but to guide you in working together with the school as a team to help your child succeed.

As you work with the activities described in this book, keep in mind that endless drilling is not the best way to help your child improve. While most children want to do well and please their teachers and parents, they already spend about seven hours a day in school. Extracurricular activities, homework, music, and sports practice take up more time. Consequently, try to use the activities in this book to stimulate and support your child's work at school without overwhelming him.

As your child enters first grade, remember that not all children learn things at the same rate. What may be typical for one first grader is certainly not for another. Thus, you should use the information presented in this book only in conjunction with your child's school work. Used accordingly, this book can be very helpful in developing your child's essential skills in reading, grammar, and writing.

How to Use This Book

Some children are quite strong in certain verbal areas, but need help in others. Perhaps your child is a whiz at understanding pictures but has trouble with reading comprehension. To use this book effectively, focus your attention and time on those skills that need some work.

You'll see in each chapter an introductory explanation of the material in the chapter, followed by a summary of what a typical child in first grade should be expected to know about that skill by the end of the year. This is followed in each chapter by an extensive section featuring interesting, fun, or unusual activities you can do with your child to reinforce the skills presented in the chapter. Most activities use only inexpensive items found around the home, and many are suitable for car trips, waiting rooms, and restaurants. Next, you'll find an explanation of how typical standardized tests may assess that skill and what your child might expect to see on a typical test.

We've included sample questions at the end of each section that are designed to help familiarize your child with the types of questions found on a typical standardized test. These questions do **not** measure your child's proficiency in any given content area. However, if you notice your child is having trouble with a particular question, you can use that information to figure out what skills you need to focus on.

Basic Test-Taking Strategies

Sometimes children score lower on standardized tests because they approach testing in an inefficient way. There are things you can do before the test—and that your child can do during the test—to make sure he does as well as he can.

Before the Test

Perhaps the most effective step you can take to prepare your child for standardized tests is to be patient. Remember that no matter how much pressure you put on your child, he won't learn certain skills until he's physically, mentally, and emotionally ready to do so. You've got to walk a delicate line between challenging and pressuring your child. If you see that your child isn't making progress or is getting frustrated, it may be time to lighten up.

Don't Change the Routine. Many experts offer mistaken advice about how to prepare children for a test, such as recommending that children go to bed early the night before or eat a high-protein breakfast on the morning of the test. In fact, you'll be better off if you don't change your child's routine at all right before the test. If your child isn't used to going to bed early, then sending him off at 7:30 p.m. the night before a test will only make it harder for him to get to sleep by the normal time. If he is used to eating an orange or a piece of toast for breakfast, forcing him to down a platter of fried eggs and bacon will only make him feel sleepy or uncomfortable.

Neatness. There is an incorrect way to fill in an answer sheet on a standardized test. If your child doesn't fill in the answer sheets correctly, this can really make a difference on the final results. It pays to give your child some practice filling in the bubbles on answer sheets. Watch how neatly your child can fill in the bubbles, squares, and rectangles below. If he overlaps the lines, makes a lot of erase marks, or presses the pencil too hard, try having him practice with pages of bubbles. You can easily create sheets of capital *O*'s, squares, and rectangles that your child can practice filling in. If he gets bored doing that, have him color in detailed pictures in coloring books or complete connect-the-dots pages.

During the Test

There are some approaches to standardized testing that have been shown to make some degree of improvement in test scores. Discuss the following strategies with your child from time to time.

Bring Extra Pencils. You don't want your child spending valuable testing time jumping up to sharpen a pencil. Send along plenty of extra, well-sharpened pencils so that your child will have more time to work on test questions.

Listen Carefully. You wouldn't believe how many errors kids make by not listening to instructions or not paying attention to demonstrations. Some children mark the wrong form, fill in the bubbles incorrectly, or skip to the wrong section. Others simply forget to put their name on the answer sheets. Many make a mark on the answer sheet without realizing they are marking the wrong bubble.

Read the Entire Question First. Some children get so excited about the test that they begin filling in bubbles before they finish reading the entire question. The last few words in a question sometimes give the most important clues to the correct answer.

Read Carefully. In their desire to finish first, many children tend to select the first answer that seems right to them without thoroughly reading all the responses and choosing the very best answer. Make sure your child understands the importance of evaluating all the answers before choosing one.

Skip Difficult Items; Return to Them Later. Many children will sit and worry about a hard question, spending so much time on one problem that they never get to problems that they would be able to answer correctly if they only had enough time. Explain to your child that he can always return to a knotty question once he finishes the section.

Refer to Pictures for Clues. Tell your child not to overlook the pictures in the test booklets, because they may reveal valuable clues he can use to help him find the correct answers. Students can also find clues to correct answers by looking carefully at the wording of the questions.

Identify Key Words. Have your child identify key words in the questions to help him figure out which parts are important and which are not.

Eliminate Answer Choices. Just like the wildly successful TV show *Who Wants to Be a Millionaire,* remind your child that it's a good idea to narrow down his choices among multiple-choice options by eliminating answers he knows can't possibly be true.

On to the Second Chapter

Now that you've learned about the test-taking basics, it's time to turn your attention to the first of the reading skills—word recognition.

CHAPTER 2

Word Analysis

The early years in school are a time of tremendous brain development. Parents who agonized over whether their child would ever learn her letters or begin to read suddenly find Jo-ann developing these skills. Unfortunately, too many parents are so concerned about reading ability that they push their children to learn to read before they are neurologically ready to do so. Many children this age are ready to read—but some children aren't. Pushing your child to start reading before she's ready will not help and can set the stage for significant frustration. If you find yourself trying to teach skills over and over, it may be that you're trying to teach a skill for which your child simply isn't ready.

What First Graders Should Know

Before a child can learn to read, she must be able to recognize and decode individual printed words—a task called *word analysis*. As a child develops this ability, along with a solid vocabulary, she will begin to be able to read independently.

By the start of first grade, you can expect your child to know the alphabet, although it may take the alphabet song to get her through it! Beginning first graders commonly need the crutch of the song to remember all the letters; many also think of some letters all in one breath, such as "ellemenohpea" (*L, M, N, O,* and *P*). You may also find that your first grader confuses some similar letters, such as *p* and *q*. This is normal and nothing to be alarmed about.

You can expect an entering first grader to be able to recognize all the uppercase letters (lowercase letters may still be a mystery, however). However, by the end of first grade, your child should know the entire alphabet in both uppercase and lowercase.

What You and Your Child Can Do

As you read through these chapters, you may notice that some activities are suggested over and over again. This is because your child won't develop some skills in isolation; many strategies are used to reinforce a wide range of skills, such as vocabulary, spelling, word recognition, picture recognition, and reading comprehension.

Read and Read Some More! The best way for your child to develop an effective vocabulary is for you to read to her. Read every day, and let her read aloud to you as well. Choose books for her on a wide range of subjects, and let your child choose some books on her own too. Be alert for her special hobbies or interests, and then provide books on that topic. Of course, you don't have to buy books—you can borrow as many books as your child can read from the local library. Encourage your child to read on her own too, and let her see you read for pleasure.

Talk. Reading isn't the only way to develop your child's word analysis skills. The more you talk to your child—and listen to what she says—the better her word analysis skills will develop. Remember, we all learn our language not from textbooks but from hearing our parents talk to us. Model proper language usage for your child.

Take a Trip. You don't have to journey to Paris to find interesting places to take your first grader. Instead, go on many local "family field trips"—to a museum, planetarium, or zoo—and encourage her to read the materials available.

Follow the Words. Most little children enjoy looking at the pictures in picture books while someone reads the story to them. Now that your child is a bit older, let her follow along and point out the words as you read. Run your finger along the words as you read. After a while, your child will come to associate the printed text with the pictures. Following the words with your finger will also reinforce to your child that in English, we read from left to right. This may seem obvious to you, but you'd be surprised at the number of children who try to read from right to left. While you read, make a special effort to point out contractions, compound words, word families, or high-frequency words.

I Want to Read! When your first grader wants to read to you, let her! Try not to be too critical, especially if your child is unsure about her budding reading ability. If your child can't read out loud for long periods, try switching—you read a page, then let her read a page.

What Tests May Ask

Tests will assess word analysis skills according to how well your child can recognize letters and their sounds. Questions often present model letters in uppercase block letters with possible answers all in lowercase.

Practice Skill: Letter Recognition

Directions: Choose the correct answers for the following questions.

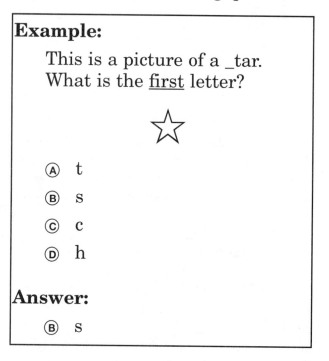

Example:

This is a picture of a _tar. What is the <u>first</u> letter?

  Ⓐ t

  Ⓑ s

  Ⓒ c

  Ⓓ h

Answer:

  Ⓑ s

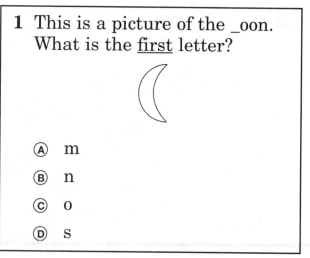

1 This is a picture of the _oon. What is the <u>first</u> letter?

  Ⓐ m

  Ⓑ n

  Ⓒ o

  Ⓓ s

2 This is a picture of a ca_. What is the <u>last</u> letter?

Ⓐ p

Ⓑ b

Ⓒ t

Ⓓ h

3 This is a picture of a _oy. What is the <u>first</u> letter?

Ⓐ p

Ⓑ g

Ⓒ b

Ⓓ y

4 Here is part of the alphabet: B C D E F _ H I J. Which letter is missing?

Ⓐ B

Ⓑ P

Ⓒ G

Ⓓ C

5 Which of these pairs of letters shows <u>different</u> letters?

Ⓐ b B

Ⓑ c C

Ⓒ q P

Ⓓ q Q

6 Which of these pairs of letters shows the <u>same</u> letters?

Ⓐ q P

Ⓑ p Q

Ⓒ d B

Ⓓ b B

(See page 87 for answer key.)

CHAPTER 3

Vocabulary

If your child is going to be a strong reader and writer, he must have a good vocabulary. By first grade, the part of the brain that controls vocabulary is developing at a furious pace. There's a lot you can do at home to boost the acquisition of words, both through the language you use and in fun games you play together.

In first grade, your child will increase the number of words he recognizes when he hears them (*receptive vocabulary*) and the number of words he uses when he speaks (*expressive vocabulary*). Typically, your child first develops receptive vocabulary because it's easier to understand language than it is to speak it. A child's receptive vocabulary is usually more fully developed than his expressive vocabulary, but as he gets older, the gap between the two diminishes.

What First Graders Should Know

Your child probably entered first grade with about 2500 words in his oral vocabulary. However, the number of words he recognizes is far greater than that. Most first graders also have a well-developed *picture vocabulary*—that is, the words they recognize from their pictures, which is a very important skill when it comes to learning how to read.

When you first started reading to your child, he learned how to associate the pictures with the words you read. Eventually, their ability to associate words and pictures leads to the ability to read without pictures. Early first graders are used to learning words by associating them with pictures. If your child sees a picture of a cat with the word *cat* beneath it, eventually he will come to understand that the word *cat* is a representation of the thing—a cat.

What You and Your Child Can Do

Read and Read Some More! The best way to help your child develop an effective vocabulary is to read to him. Read to him every day, and let him read aloud to you. Encourage your child to read on his own, too, and let him see you read for pleasure.

Play Commercial Games. There are many commercial games that are good for boosting vocabulary. Games such as *Password* or *Scrabble Junior* are old favorites and can help boost vocabulary (although you will need to simplify and modify the rules so that they are appropriate for a first grader's ability).

Obtain and Use a Beginning Thesaurus. Parents may want to consider buying a "beginner's thesaurus" to help children develop essential literary skills needed for writing and reading.

Play Thumper. Players sit around a table thumping the tabletop in a rhythm. The first child calls out a category name (such as "fruits"). Then play proceeds around the table as each child calls out something from that category, such as "pineapples" or "bananas" before a prearranged number of thumps have passed. The first player who can't name an item from the category (or who calls out something someone already has given) is "out." The final player left wins.

2046272

Take a Trip. You don't have to journey to London to find interesting places to take your first grader. Take regular outings to a local museum, planetarium, or zoo and encourage him to read the materials available. A curious child with lots of stimulation will almost automatically increase his vocabulary. If your child is interested in horses, take him to a local stable to watch what goes on. If he's interested in animals, visit the zoo and join the volunteer zoo society. The more he is exposed to and reads about the things that interest him, the better his vocabulary will be.

Talk. Your child's vocabulary will improve the more time you spend talking to him. Even though your family's schedule, like most families, is hectic at times, try to spend some time around the family dinner table sharing the day's activities and discussing current events. Make sure everyone gets a chance to be heard—even the littlest first grader.

Build a Scaffold. One good way to boost your child's use of words is to build a verbal "scaffold" by using a complex word and then defining it in simpler terms right afterward. For example: Lauren's mother might say, "That bird's feathers are iridescent. They shine and reflect the sun's rays." Children with the biggest vocabularies tend to have parents who automatically scaffold their sentences.

Define It. Of course, it's also helpful to simply define words outright: "Let's get that medicine in the *pharmacy*. A *pharmacy* is a place that sells medicine. It's also called a *drugstore*." Don't automatically use the simplest words when you talk to your child, and avoid baby talk. Instead, speak to him as if he were older. You might be surprised at how his vocabulary improves in response.

Play Hangman. This popular family game requires just a pencil and a scrap of paper—a great diversion during endless waits in the doctor's office or a restaurant. When it's your turn to give a word, don't use the simplest word you can think of. Instead, use a more challenging choice, and explain the word once the child has guessed all the letters.

Play Catalog Find. Most young children enjoy looking through catalogs (especially toy catalogs). Have your child cut out catalog pictures and paste them onto index cards to make your own set of flash cards. Have your child print the word that describes the picture underneath.

Look It Up. Invest in a good child's dictionary, and help your child look up words in it. Let him see you look up words you don't understand in your dictionary too. On a rainy day, set a timer, and have two children compete to see who can look up a word the fastest.

What's Happening? There are a number of beautifully illustrated books with no words at all. Look through these books with your child, encouraging him to discuss what might be going on in the pictures.

Play Photo Find. One good way to develop picture vocabulary is to get out the family photo album. Children love looking at photos (especially pictures of themselves). As you turn the page, ask your first grader: What are you doing in this picture?

Write a Story. Here's a good rainy-day activity if your child has a friend over to play. Have one child draw a series of pictures on several sheets of paper and staple them together (or cut out pictures from a magazine and paste them on paper). Have the other child write a story by printing a few words to go with each picture. The writer will need to study the pictures carefully. Then have the two children switch places.

Play Word Scramble. This popular party game can be lots of fun for children to play, especially if you get several children together and offer a prize to the player who finds the most words. In word scramble, choose one large word (such as *Halloween*), and have children find as many smaller words within the large word as they can. Set a time limit.

What Tests May Ask

Standardized tests for first graders assess vocabulary development in several ways. Tests may present sentences with a word missing and ask a child to fill in the blank with a correct word from a group of choices. They will assess picture vocabulary by asking the child to name or recognize objects that he sees in pictures. To assess expressive picture vocabulary, a test question may ask a child to look at a picture and then choose the word that describes what the subject of the picture is doing. To test receptive picture vocabulary, a child may be asked to read a word and then choose one picture out of a group of pictures that represents that word.

Practice Skill: Vocabulary

Directions: Choose the correct word to go in the blank in the following sentences.

Example:

The dog chased a _____.

Ⓐ tree

Ⓑ car

Ⓒ hole

Ⓓ grass

Answer:

Ⓑ car

1 Mother sent Billy to the _____ to buy some milk.

Ⓐ school

Ⓑ office

Ⓒ store

Ⓓ house

2 Sharon could not _____ her lost book.

Ⓐ hear

Ⓑ eat

Ⓒ find

Ⓓ lose

3 It gets dark at _____.

Ⓐ night

Ⓑ day

Ⓒ cow

Ⓓ school

17

Directions: Look at each picture and choose the correct answer from the choices given below.

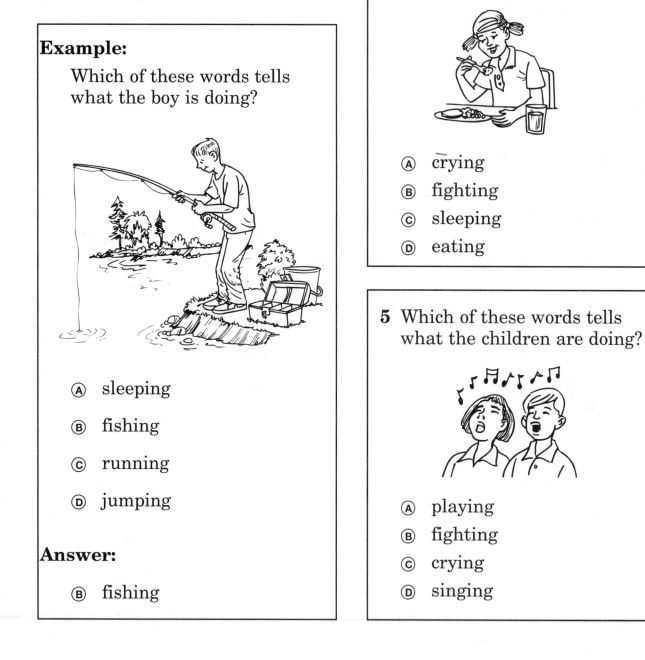

Example:

Which of these words tells what the boy is doing?

Ⓐ sleeping

Ⓑ fishing

Ⓒ running

Ⓓ jumping

Answer:

Ⓑ fishing

4 Which of these words tells what the girl is doing?

Ⓐ crying

Ⓑ fighting

Ⓒ sleeping

Ⓓ eating

5 Which of these words tells what the children are doing?

Ⓐ playing

Ⓑ fighting

Ⓒ crying

Ⓓ singing

6 Which of these words tells what the dog is doing?

- Ⓐ sleeping
- Ⓑ barking
- Ⓒ jumping
- Ⓓ eating

7 Where is Fluffy the cat hiding?

- Ⓐ in the trees
- Ⓑ in the dog house
- Ⓒ in the bedroom
- Ⓓ in the attic

8 Which picture shows the children running?

Ⓐ
Ⓑ
Ⓒ
Ⓓ

9 Which picture shows the dog playing?

(See page 87 for answer key.)

CHAPTER 4

Synonyms, Antonyms, and Homophones

If your child is to develop a good vocabulary, she must understand how words relate to other words as synonyms, antonyms, and homophones. A basic understanding of "alike" and "different" is so vital to being a good reader that these concepts will be included on most standardized tests.

Synonyms

A *synonym* is a word that means *the same as* another word. *Big* and *large* are examples of synonyms that first graders can grasp. Most children this age can understand that two separate words can mean the same thing. First graders love playing with words in this way, and they enjoy games in which they must try to come up with as many synonyms as possible.

What First Graders Should Know

While most first graders can understand the fact that two different words can mean the same thing, most won't yet understand the term *synonym*. They can be quite accurate with simple comparisons, however. Most first graders will emphasize concrete similarities.

What You and Your Child Can Do

Same As! Playing word games with synonyms can be lots of fun and simple to do at home. If your child has trouble remembering what a synonym is, explain that *synonym* and *same as* both begin with the same letter: *s*.

Top It! This game is great to play any time, because you don't need any props. Try it during a long wait at a restaurant or the doctor's office. One player starts off with a simple sentence: "I'm big." The next person tries to "top the phrase"—"I'm gigantic!" The first person then counters: "I'm HUGE!" The second person then says: "I'm humongous!" The game continues until no one can think of any more synonyms for the one word. Then you can begin all over again with new words.

Concentration. This game requires preparation, but once the cards are made, you can play the game over and over.

1. Take a stack of 10 index cards, and print a pair of synonyms on each card, such as *big* and *large*.

2. Cut each card in two to separate the synonyms.

3. Mix them up and turn them face down on a table.

4. One by one, each player turns over two cards. If the two cards are synonyms, the player gets to keep the cards. If they are not, she turns the cards over face down again, and play continues to the next player.

5. At the end of the game, the player with the most cards wins.

Guessing Games. These games make good car entertainment, as they don't require pencil or paper. Start off this way:

YOU: I'm thinking of a word whose synonym means "big."

CHILD: Large!

YOU: No, that's not it.

CHILD: Tall!

YOU: Good guess, but not the word I'm thinking of.

CHILD: Gigantic!

YOU: That's it!

Rephrasing. Children don't learn just from reading books—they learn as much from talking to you on an everyday basis. When you're chatting, try rephrasing to expand your child's vocabulary:

CHILD: What a cute puppy!

YOU: Yes, that puppy is really *adorable,* isn't he!

What Tests May Ask

Standardized tests for first graders will assess a child's understanding of similarities in several ways. Some questions may ask your child to choose a synonym for an underlined word in a sentence from among a group of possibilities. Other questions may present groups of two words and ask your child to choose the pair in which the words mean the same thing. Then your child may be asked to choose a pair in which the words do *not* mean the same thing. All these variations on the synonym theme are trying to make sure your child understands that it's possible for two different words to carry the same meaning.

Practice Skill: Synonyms

Directions: Look at the underlined word in each sentence. Which word is a **synonym** (a word that means the same thing) for the underlined word?

Example:

I'm <u>glad</u> the storm is over.

Ⓐ happy

Ⓑ afraid

Ⓒ sorry

Ⓓ mad

Answer:

Ⓐ happy

---

1 My friend was <u>mad</u> when she lost her book.

Ⓐ happy

Ⓑ angry

Ⓒ sad

Ⓓ good

---

2 Sam <u>raced</u> down the stairs.

Ⓐ jumped

Ⓑ hopped

Ⓒ ran

Ⓓ walked

---

3 The rabbit <u>jumped</u> over the rock.

Ⓐ fell

Ⓑ hopped

Ⓒ ran

Ⓓ walked

Directions: Choose the pair of words below in which the words mean the same thing.

Example:

- Ⓐ walk   run
- Ⓑ close   near
- Ⓒ dog   horse
- Ⓓ go   stop

Answer:

- Ⓑ close   near

4 Ⓐ red   white
- Ⓑ slip   slide
- Ⓒ fast   slow
- Ⓓ run   walk

5 Ⓐ peas   carrots
- Ⓑ sing   talk
- Ⓒ eat   drink
- Ⓓ quick   fast

6 Ⓐ round   flat
- Ⓑ glad   happy
- Ⓒ green   blue
- Ⓓ penny   dime

(See page 87 for answer key.)

Antonyms

An *antonym* is a word that means the opposite of another word. While first graders may not know the term, they do understand the concept and they are intrigued by words that mean the opposite of other words.

What First Graders Should Know

Your first grader probably lacks a certain depth of understanding when it comes to opposites; her comprehension of differences among words is probably limited to concrete comparisons that rely on tangible properties, such as *up* versus *down*.

What You and Your Child Can Do

Computer Games. There are many fine educational software programs out there that teach a wide variety of language arts skills. *Jump Start First Grade* (Knowledge Adventure) is one good example that includes a wide variety of fun activities. In the game that teaches synonyms and antonyms, students match words to help other children in the class find lost items.

Antonym Matching Game. In this game, a twist on the old "concentration" game, your child will be matching up opposites instead of synonyms:

1. Gather a stack of 10 index cards and write antonyms, one on each half of the index card.

2. Cut apart the two words on each index card.

3. Turn them face down on a table, and arrange them in five lines, two cards to a line.

4. Have the first child turn over two cards. If they are antonyms, she gets to keep the cards. If not, she turns the cards face down again, and the next player begins. The

player with the most cards at the end wins the game.

Opposite Day. Speak in opposites for this word game—"I was up really late last night. Now I'm really awake." instead of "Now I'm really tired." Or "That hamburger really made me hungry." instead of "That hamburger really filled me up."

Antonym Bingo. Here's a fun twist on an old favorite. Make your own antonym bingo cards using antonym pairs appropriate for a first grader. Remember to keep them concrete: *bad/good, big/little, buy/sell, cold/hot, dark/light, mad/happy, early/late, more/less, open/close, back/front, rich/poor, sick/well, slow/fast, soft/hard, tall/short,* and *young/old.* Then make the game boards:

1. Cut game boards from thick paper, and draw bingo grids of 20 equal squares.

2. Print the first words of the antonym pairs on the game boards (make each board different).

3. Print the matching word of each antonym pair on index cards.

4. Each player chooses a game board and 10 chips.

5. The leader reads a word from the deck of index cards. Each player looks on her game board for the matching antonyms. If she finds a match, she covers the word with a chip.

6. The first player to cover a row horizontally, diagonally, or vertically calls out "bingo!"

Defining New Words. The next time your child asks you the meaning of a new word, include the antonym as well as the definition or synonym:

CHILD: What does *wealthy* mean?

YOU: *Wealthy* means the same as *rich*. The opposite of *wealthy* is *poor*.

Riddles. The next time you go on a family trip, try making up a riddle for your child to solve

using antonyms: "I mean the opposite of 'short,' and I rhyme with 'fall.'" Not only will your child learn about antonyms, she'll learn how to analyze words, too.

What Tests May Ask

Standardized tests for first graders will assess a child's understanding of opposites in much the same way that synonyms are measured, and in a very concrete way. Some questions may ask your child to choose an antonym for an underlined word in a sentence from a group of possibilities. Some tests may present two words and ask your child to choose the pair in which the words mean the opposite. Your child may be asked to choose a pair in which the words *do* mean the same thing. All these variations are designed to make sure your child is able to recognize opposite words.

Practice Skill: Antonyms

Directions: Look at each sentence and pick the word that means the **opposite** of the word that is underlined.

Example:

Jim did not get up on time. He is going to be <u>late</u>.

Ⓐ mad

Ⓑ glad

Ⓒ early

Ⓓ sick

Answer:

Ⓒ early

7 Kara forgot to <u>close</u> the door.

- (A) clean
- (B) shut
- (C) call
- (D) open

8 I want to <u>buy</u> a new toy.

- (A) sell
- (B) get
- (C) eat
- (D) run

9 At midnight it is very <u>dark</u>.

- (A) thick
- (B) black
- (C) light
- (D) late

Directions: Choose the pair in which the words are opposite in meaning.

Example:

- (A) run   race
- (B) slow   fast
- (C) green   white
- (D) push   eat

Answer:

- (B) slow   fast

10

- (A) ears   mouth
- (B) push   pull
- (C) in   down
- (D) house   bed

11

- (A) cold   cool
- (B) in   out
- (C) hop   jump
- (D) cat   kitten

12

- (A) fast   quick
- (B) bad   good
- (C) small   tiny
- (D) big   huge

(See page 87 for answer key.)

Homophones

Homophones are a little more difficult than synonyms and antonyms for a first grader to understand. A *homophone* is a word that sounds the same as another word but may be spelled differently and have a different meaning. An example of two homophones are *I* and *eye*. It's important for children to recognize that the words sound the same but may have different spellings for the two meanings.

What First Graders Should Know

Your first grader should have a basic understanding of homophones. She should be able to decide which homophone correctly fits in a sentence, and recognize homophones in reading and writing. She should also be able to come up with some examples of homophone pairs.

You may need to help your child understand that, in some cases, homophones may not be spelled differently. For example, the word *orange* can mean a color or a fruit. This is when your child needs to pay close attention to how the word is used in context.

What You and Your Child Can Do

Concentration. This game requires preparation, but once the cards are made, you can play the game over and over.

1. Take a stack of 10 index cards, and print a pair of homophones on each card, such as *hear* and *here*.

2. Cut each card in two to separate the homophones.

3. Mix them up and turn them face down on a table.

4. One by one, each player turns over two cards. If the two cards are a pair of homophones, the player gets to keep the cards. If they are not, the player turns the cards over face down again, and play continues to the next player.

5. At the end of the game, the player with the most cards wins.

Do You Hear What I Hear? If your child is having trouble remembering what a homophone is, tell her that *homophone* begins with an *h* and so does the word *hear*. This will help her make the connection with homophones and the fact that they sound the same.

Which One Belongs? You can use the same cards for this activity that you made for the homophone concentration game. In this version, you can make up sentences that use homophones. Give your child a pair of homophones, and read her a sentence that uses one of the words in the pair. Have your child listen to the sentence and show you which one of the words fits into the sentence correctly.

Pick One. Write down homophone pairs on cards. Put the cards in a hat or bag, and let your child draw a card. Have your child use each one of the homophones on her card in a sentence correctly.

What Tests May Ask

Standardized tests may not directly ask questions about homophones, but children need to have a basic understanding of homophones to apply to other areas of tests. Children will be asked to correctly choose words that correspond with pictures, and homophones may be included in the answer choices. Children may also be asked to correctly fill in the blanks of sentences. This task would also require a basic knowledge of homophones. If homophones are included in the answer choices, choosing the wrong word would alter the intended meaning of the sentence. If tests were to ask a direct question relating to homophones, they would probably give children a word and require them to choose the correct word to complete the homophone pair.

Practice Skill: Homophones

Directions: Look at the picture in each question. Which word correctly corresponds with the picture? Make sure you pay close attention to the spellings of the words.

Example:

2

- Ⓐ to
- Ⓑ top
- Ⓒ two
- Ⓓ too

Answer:

- Ⓒ two

13

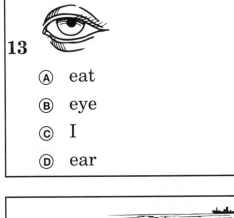

- Ⓐ eat
- Ⓑ eye
- Ⓒ I
- Ⓓ ear

14

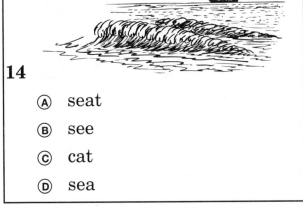

- Ⓐ seat
- Ⓑ see
- Ⓒ cat
- Ⓓ sea

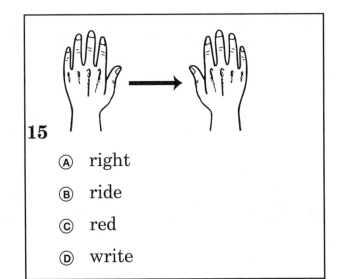

15

- Ⓐ right
- Ⓑ ride
- Ⓒ red
- Ⓓ write

Directions: Choose the word (or words) that correctly fits into the sentence.

Example:

I _____ up a balloon.

- Ⓐ boy
- Ⓑ blue
- Ⓒ bat
- Ⓓ blew

Answer:

- Ⓓ blew

16 I walked _____ the store.

- Ⓐ two
- Ⓑ top
- Ⓒ to
- Ⓓ too

17 My soccer team _____ the game.

- Ⓐ won
- Ⓑ two
- Ⓒ on
- Ⓓ one

18 I _____ a book called *Clifford, The Big* _____ *Dog.*

- Ⓐ red, Happy
- Ⓑ read, Red
- Ⓒ have, Read
- Ⓓ red, Read

(See page 87 for answer key.)

CHAPTER 5

Word Meanings in Context

In first grade, children increase their vocabulary and word-attack skills in a dramatic way as they begin to learn how to read. Most adults take reading for granted, without thinking about the process. But first graders are just starting to put all the pieces of the puzzle together. It's important to realize the significance of reading in context. While you read individual sentences one by one, you don't focus on each word individually, as if it had no relationship to the words around it. Instead, you read *in context*—as one complete whole.

When a child first learns to put words together, he doesn't look at a sentence as an unbroken whole. Instead, most children learn to read by identifying "chunks" of words or picking out basic sight words that they recognize. Your child may slowly increase the pace and flow of his reading. Only later will he begin to see words in the context of entire sentences.

An integrated language program should emphasize the fact that a child in first grade needs to understand the meaning of individual words as they are used within an entire selection, in addition to their meaning when they stand alone. By using words in sentences, children can make sure they have decoded the words correctly. Understanding the context of a word can also help a child figure out an unknown word and make sure that he doesn't confuse the word with a similar-looking or similar-sounding word.

What First Graders Should Know

When your child first began to read out loud, his reading probably sounded mechanical. His monotone voice was a result of his reading by sounding out individual words. Often when a beginner reads a word incorrectly, he keeps on going even if the sentence isn't making a bit of sense. Early readers tend to read words or parts of the sentence individually, without an overall sense of the total meaning of the sentence.

Working on helping your child read in context will ultimately make him a better reader and help develop his reading comprehension. You can also help your child as he reads by having him ask questions at the end of a sentence that he may have misread. (Do the words I read look right and sound right according to what is printed on the page? Does the sentence make sense? Do the picture clues on the page match with what I just read?)

Helping your child achieve these skills will promote self-correction as he becomes a more confident reader.

What You and Your Child Can Do

Preview the Story. Take a picture walk and help your child decide what words he thinks might be on the page. If your child says a word that's on the page, show the word to your child.

Knowing a few words ahead of time will help your child have a sense of the story.

Read! Reading to your child—and having him read to you—will increase his ability to understand words in context. If he comes to a word he doesn't understand, have him stop to see if he can puzzle out its meaning from the context of the sentence. Let him see how the sentence as a whole relates. Read poems out loud. Point to the words on the page as you read.

Have Fun with Sentences. While you're waiting to be served in a restaurant, try to work on context this way: Give your child a sentence with a word missing. See how many words he can think of that would fit in the blank and still make sense. Talk with your child about which words seem to be the most logical fit.

I Read, You Read. You read a section of print, and your child reads that same section as an echo. This will help you model phrasing, expression, and fluency.

Reread. When your child reads a word incorrectly out loud, let him read to the end of the sentence to see if he can correct the mistake just from the meaning of the sentence. If he can't, have him go back to the beginning of the sentence and read it again. This will help your child become a better reader by listening to what he's reading to make sure it makes sense.

What Tests May Ask

Most standardized tests will assess your child's ability to understand the meaning of words as they are used in context. The tests will offer a sentence and ask your child to fill in the blank with the word that makes the most sense. This requires your child to understand what words do and don't fit into a sentence given a sentence's meaning. It also means your child must understand that a word may have more than one meaning and that not properly decoding a word can change the meaning of a sentence.

Practice Skill: Word Meanings in Context

Directions: In the following examples, read each sentence and choose the word that best fits in the blank.

Example:

It was time to do the dishes, so Ahmed ran some water into the ___.

- Ⓐ sink
- Ⓑ bed
- Ⓒ tub
- Ⓓ book

Answer:

- Ⓐ sink

1 The _____ child had the most candles on the cake.
- Ⓐ oldest
- Ⓑ strongest
- Ⓒ youngest
- Ⓓ prettiest

2 Lateesha was too _____ to reach the top shelf.
- Ⓐ tall
- Ⓑ short
- Ⓒ good
- Ⓓ bad

3 The princess could not sleep because the bed was too ___.

  Ⓐ slow

  Ⓑ sweet

  Ⓒ hard

  Ⓓ fast

4 The horse got out because Sue forgot to _____ the barn door.

  Ⓐ up

  Ⓑ down

  Ⓒ open

  Ⓓ close

5 Montrose was too _____ to stay home alone.

  Ⓐ old

  Ⓑ young

  Ⓒ rich

  Ⓓ mean

6 Jose was _____ of the snarling bear.

  Ⓐ afraid

  Ⓑ happy

  Ⓒ mad

  Ⓓ wild

Directions: In the following examples, read each sentence and choose the answer that means the same as the underlined word.

Example:

Jill was too <u>little</u> to hold the baby.

  Ⓐ big

  Ⓑ tall

  Ⓒ small

  Ⓓ bad

Answer:

  Ⓒ small

7 Elizabeth was <u>sick</u>. She had a fever.

  Ⓐ hungry

  Ⓑ good

  Ⓒ ill

  Ⓓ sad

8 We will have to run <u>fast</u> to get to school on time.

  Ⓐ slowly

  Ⓑ quickly

  Ⓒ angrily

  Ⓓ happily

Directions: Read the paragraph below. Find the word below the paragraph that best fits in each numbered blank.

Example:

Tomico had __1__ at her friend's house. The two girls played __2__ all night.

1 Ⓐ puppies
  Ⓑ fun
  Ⓒ dolphins
  Ⓓ sad

2 Ⓐ cats
  Ⓑ mothers
  Ⓒ games
  Ⓓ hats

Answers:

1 Ⓑ fun   2 Ⓒ games

Jamie and Carol spent the day at the fair. They tossed __9__ at bottles to try to knock them down. Carol won a __10__! For lunch they bought hot dogs and had a __11__ of water. The __12__ felt warm on their skin. By the end of the long, busy day, they were tired but __13__.

9 Ⓐ mud
  Ⓑ hot dogs
  Ⓒ balls
  Ⓓ coats

10 Ⓐ prize
   Ⓑ rock
   Ⓒ hat
   Ⓓ oven

11 Ⓐ test
   Ⓑ cat
   Ⓒ rain
   Ⓓ drink

12 Ⓐ tree
   Ⓑ sunshine
   Ⓒ snow
   Ⓓ pig

13 Ⓐ green
   Ⓑ mad
   Ⓒ happy
   Ⓓ old

(See page 87 for answer key.)

CHAPTER 6

Word Sounds

Being able to link the sound of a word with its consonant or vowel counterpart is the basis of phonics, which—although drifting in and out of favor over the years—is still usually taught in some fashion in all schools. The study of consonant sounds includes both beginning and ending consonant sounds (such as the C in *Cat* or the ending S in *hatS*).

Beginning and Ending Word Sounds

When it comes to learning word sounds, you'll find that most schools emphasize beginning sounds first, so expect to see lots of work on "alphabet words" (A is for *Apple,* B is for *Ball,* C is for *Cat*). It may sound simple, but figuring out a beginning sound means your child must know which sound is really the beginning sound. For the same reason, identifying ending sounds can be even more difficult for many children.

What First Graders Should Know

First graders should have a solid understanding of both beginning and ending sounds, vowel sounds, and rhyming sounds. They should be able to listen for the beginning and ending sounds, recognize long and short vowel sounds separately, use beginning consonants to figure out new words, and recognize and create rhyming sounds.

But don't be surprised if your child gets confused by many word ending sounds, in part because of confusion over the word *ending.*

Ending sounds tend to present more of a challenge than beginning sounds for early first graders. When asked to name ending sounds, many children name the beginning sound instead. There may be a developmental reason for this confusion, but starting at about age 6, children will benefit from practicing ending sound skills.

What You and Your Child Can Do

Reading. Reading to your child is probably the best all-around way to help her become a good reader, and it certainly helps in working on beginning and ending word sounds. But don't just read to your child—help her follow along as you read the words on the page. Point to a word as you say it.

Grandmother's House. This is a great game for long car rides—and it not only works to boost memory skills, but it also helps reinforce beginning word sounds. The first player starts off the game by choosing an object beginning with the first letter of the alphabet. The next player repeats the first sentence and then adds an object using the second letter of the alphabet.

CHILD: I went to Grandmother's house and I took an Apple.

YOU: I went to Grandmother's house, and I took an Apple and a Bat.

CHILD: I went to Grandmother's house, and I took an Apple, a Bat, and a Caterpillar.

Magazine Find. Let your child choose a consonant (or draw one from a bag of scrabble tiles or magnetic letters). Then go through magazines, and ask her to find pictures of everything that begins with that letter.

Treasure Hunt. Send your child off on a treasure hunt for items that begin with a consonant you choose. For example, C might result in: *Cat, Coat, Cookie.*

What Tests May Ask

Standardized tests will include questions on both beginning and ending consonant sounds. Questions may attempt to distract the child with similar sounds, which may well trip up first graders. In assessing a child's understanding of beginning and ending sounds, tests may ask questions that require the child to be able to recognize which sound of a word is the beginning or ending sound. If your child has trouble with this type of task, encourage her to say the words aloud to determine the beginning and ending sounds.

For first graders, the tests will probably include a range of easier items through more difficult questions assessing ending sounds. Questions will typically present several answers with somewhat similar ending sounds, with at least one choice using the same beginning sound as the ending sound that the child needs to find.

Practice Skill: Beginning Word Sounds

Directions: Read each question and choose the correct answer.

Example:

In which pair do the words **begin** with the same sound?

- Ⓐ ball   pat
- Ⓑ city   cat
- Ⓒ car   kid
- Ⓓ go   jump

Answer:

- Ⓒ car   kid

---

1 In which pair do the words **begin** with the same sound?

- Ⓐ horse   house
- Ⓑ ball   pen
- Ⓒ hair   nose
- Ⓓ can   chin

---

2 In which pair do the words **begin** with the same sound?

- Ⓐ fun   sun
- Ⓑ go   jump
- Ⓒ goat   get
- Ⓓ dog   cat

3 *G* is for *Goat.* *H* is for *Horse.* *J* is for *Jelly.* What is *K* for?

Ⓐ church

Ⓑ sun

Ⓒ sat

Ⓓ kid

4 Choose the word that begins with the same sound as the word in the picture below.

Ⓐ boots

Ⓑ seat

Ⓒ lamb

Ⓓ glass

Practice Skill: Ending Word Sounds

Directions: Read each question and choose the correct answer.

Example:

Which of these words has the same **ending** sound as in the word <u>cat</u>?

Ⓐ can

Ⓑ sit

Ⓒ sip

Ⓓ case

Answer:

Ⓑ sit

5 Choose the pair in which the words have the same **ending** sound.

Ⓐ sat   foot

Ⓑ sun   car

Ⓒ big   lick

Ⓓ show   hard

6 Which of these words has a different **ending** sound than the others?

Ⓐ rip

Ⓑ rug

Ⓒ rap

Ⓓ tap

7 Here is a fish. Which word has the same **ending** sound as <u>fish</u>?

Ⓐ witch

Ⓑ dish

Ⓒ crack

Ⓓ safe

Directions: Choose the ending letter that makes the ending sound for each picture following.

Example:

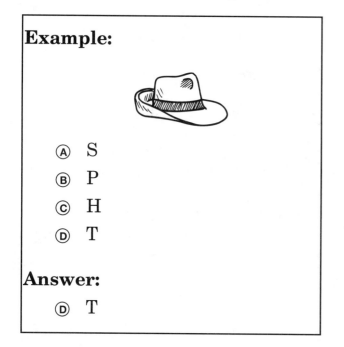

- Ⓐ S
- Ⓑ P
- Ⓒ H
- Ⓓ T

Answer:

- Ⓓ T

8 Ⓐ D
  Ⓑ T
  Ⓒ G
  Ⓓ S

(See page 87 for answer key.)

Vowel Sounds

English is a language with complicated and sometimes unpredictable rules for vowel sounds that can be quite difficult for early readers to puzzle out. The parts of the brain that govern sophisticated vowel sounds undergo tremendous development beginning at age 6.

What First Graders Should Know

The difference between vowel and consonant sounds will probably be foreign to beginning first graders, even until the end of the first year. It's fairly common for even late first graders to be unable to label "vowel" versus "consonant" sounds, although by the end of first grade many will be able to mimic the *oo* sound or to understand that the letter A has both a short sound (as in *cat*) and a long sound as in *ate*—the "vowel that says its name."

What You and Your Child Can Do

Vowel Game. While you're driving in the car, try out this game: Ask your child to come up with words for various vowel sounds:

YOU: Can you think of a word in which the A says its name, like *caaaaake*?

CHILD: Bake. Make. Take.

Rhyme Time. You can combine two types of word sounds—rhymes and vowels—in this game:

YOU: I'm thinking of a word that rhymes with *go.*

CHILD: Throw!

What Tests May Ask

You can bet that standardized tests will include questions on vowel sounds, and they may include distracting questions with similar sounds. However, by late first grade, most students should be able to identify vowel sounds so well that they can confidently pick the correct answer from similar-sounding choices.

Practice Skill: Vowel Sounds

Directions: Match the word with the same vowel sound as the underlined word in each question.

Example:

Which word has the same **vowel** sound as in hoot?

Ⓐ boot

Ⓑ hop

Ⓒ nap

Ⓓ hip

Answer:

Ⓐ boot

9 What word has the same **vowel** sound as in feet?

Ⓐ beet

Ⓑ red

Ⓒ fed

Ⓓ bed

10 Which word has the same **vowel** sound as in coat?

Ⓐ head

Ⓑ toad

Ⓒ cat

Ⓓ cool

11 Which word has the same **vowel** sound as mile?

Ⓐ man

Ⓑ mat

Ⓒ ride

Ⓓ moon

(See page 87 for answer key.)

Rhyming Sounds

Rhyming sounds are lots of fun for first graders, and the sillier the rhyme, the better they like it. However, many first graders find it quite confusing that different letters or combinations make the same sounds. It may be hard for youngsters this age to see that *wait* and *eight* rhyme when they see them written.

What First Graders Should Know

The concept of rhyming sounds is a difficult one, and many children won't fully grasp this idea until second to early third grade. Nevertheless, many standardized tests in first grade will have a few questions on rhyming words. By sounding out the word, first graders should begin to hear which words can rhyme.

What You and Your Child Can Do

Write a Poem. Many first graders love poems because with poetry, they can express themselves without needing to worry about punctuation, complete sentences, and all those grammatical "shoulds." Take time to sit down with your child and try to paint a picture in a poem.

Read Aloud. Poems often sound best when read aloud. Read often to your first grader, and pick up a poetry book now and then. Shel Silverstein's funny verses are big favorites of this age. After you read a poem, ask your child what she likes about the poem and what the poem makes her feel or think of. Ask your child if there is a sound she notices in a particular poem. How does the poet use sound to make the poem more effective?

What Tests May Ask

Standardized tests in first grade may assess rhyming sounds by using different letters and combinations that make the same sound. Most tests will try to gauge your child's ability to recognize rhyming words by including questions in which all but the correct answer begin with the same letter. This may confuse children who are unsure of their ability to recognize rhymes. Questions also may ask your child to find the one word that does *not* rhyme with the example word.

Practice Skill: Rhyming Sounds

Directions: Choose the correct answer for the following questions.

Example:

Which of these animal names rhymes with <u>hat</u>?

Ⓐ hippo

Ⓑ bear

Ⓒ bat

Ⓓ hare

Answer:

Ⓒ bat

12 Which of these words rhymes with <u>bed</u>?

Ⓐ bad

Ⓑ bit

Ⓒ red

Ⓓ rod

13 Which of these words rhyme with <u>pen</u>?

Ⓐ pool

Ⓑ nut

Ⓒ den

Ⓓ hat

14 Which two words rhyme?

Ⓐ all, ate

Ⓑ dog, log

Ⓒ ran, run

Ⓓ goat, gull

(See page 87 for answer key.)

CHAPTER 7

Spelling

Spelling is still an important part of first grade despite the proliferation of computers equipped with spell checkers. Almost all schools use some type of basic word list of common words that students are expected to master. Ask your child's teacher for the list of words she's working on so that you will know what words your child is learning at school.

Many teachers have their own list of words that match what they're doing in class as well as lists required for the grade level. Spelling lists may include "high-frequency words," which are words used most often in English. These words are important for your child to know, since they will appear often in books and be used frequently in writing.

Because English is a blended language with so many words borrowed from other languages, learning how to spell correctly is a difficult task, and children take many years to become proficient. Even well-educated adults admit they have trouble spelling many words. English can be hard to understand because there are so many exceptions to the rules.

Some schools avoid teaching spelling in first grade out of a concern that doing so might interfere with a child's creativity. However, it's much easier to teach correct spelling in the beginning of a child's education than to correct poor spelling habits later on.

Some teachers may refer to the term *inventive spelling*. This is the spelling of words as they sound or as a child hears them. Inventive spelling is acceptable in the writing of young children that are just learning to spell and write, but as children become more confident writers and spellers, it is important for them to be exposed to the correct spelling of words. The more children see and practice using words spelled correctly, the faster they will learn them.

What First Graders Should Know

Most children when they enter first grade should already have a firm grasp of the alphabet and be familiar with the sounds that are made by each letter. By the middle of first grade, your child should be able to spell many of the high-frequency words and be familiar with some of the short-vowel, one-syllable words. Some examples of high-frequency words are *the, of, and, you, to,* and *I.* Short-vowel words are very important for your child to know, because their patterns can help children learn more than one word at a time. Short-vowel words are best taught with the use of "word families." When your child learns a word family like *-at,* they should be able to put different letters at the beginning to form many short-vowel words; for example, *b* would make *bat, c* would make *cat,* and *h* would make *hat.* By late first grade, your child should feel comfortable with spelling short-vowel words and high-frequency words. He should also be spelling some two-syllable words. When your child learns to spell new words, he should be able to recognize them in text, spell them in isolation, and use them in his writing.

What You and Your Child Can Do

Play School. If your child likes to play school, be sure to include a brief spelling session. Line up your child's stuffed animals as "classmates," and have a spelling bee—with your child spelling all the words for them. Give a little prize to the winning "bear."

Make Your Own Words. Let your child spell out words in pancake batter, jello letters, or bread, using alphabet cookie cutters.

Read! By now this activity should be second nature. The most important thing for young spellers to do is to have lots of exposure to all kinds of printed materials. The more your child sees words written, the more he will begin to develop an idea of what spelling looks "right" and which looks wrong. In fact, many good spellers can check their own spelling by writing a word several different ways; the correct spelling just looks "right" to them.

Play *Scrabble Junior.* This child-size version of the adult *Scrabble* game is a real boost to spelling. Prompts in the form of pictures and words that are spelled out on the board help your child avoid frustration.

Write in the Sand. Take an old wash basin and partially fill it with clean playground sand. Give your child a word, and let him "write" the word in the sand.

Write in Shaving Cream. If you fear that sand might be too messy, take a can of shaving cream and spread it over a washable surface. Let your child "write" spelling words in the foam. (The top of a washable kitchen table works well. Or use the shower stall during bath time, to really be on the safe side!)

Deck the Halls. Using index cards or the backs of old business cards, print simple one-word labels for common objects around your house (*bed, chair, phone, dog, dish, rug, table*). Let your child tape the labels to the appropriate items so that he will get used to linking the correctly spelled word to the item it represents.

Play Hangman. This old favorite is a wonderful way to learn spelling words. While it could be challenging for some first graders, if you keep the words short, it may be fun for your youngster.

Have your child choose a word, mark out the spaces for each letter, and then you try to guess the word your child is thinking of. Then switch, and you choose a word and let your child guess what it is. Give your child some helpful strategies: Suggest he try vowels first, since all words must have vowels. Ask him which letters are most common. If the second letter is an H, talk about what letter might go with the H—S or C, for example. You can play this game anywhere, with paper and pencil, on a chalkboard, dry erase board—even with magnetic letters on a fridge. Start with very simple, three-letter words, and increase the complexity of the words as your child improves.

Let Them Glow. Here's a good way to practice spelling words: Give your child glow-in-the-dark pens or crayons, and have him write his spelling words on white paper. Then hang up the words, and have him enjoy reading them in the dark!

Word Cut-up. Write spelling words on pieces of paper with the letters spread apart. Cut them up and let your child unscramble the letters to make the words. You can store the letters in plastic bags and use them over and over. You can even remove a letter and see if your child can figure out the word and which letter is missing.

Ghost Words. Draw frames using shapes (a rectangle for the letters that go above or dip down below the midline and squares for other letters). Make sure the shapes are hooked together so that it looks like a word. You can give your child a "word bank" of a few words to choose from. Have them decide which letter fits the frame. This activity is helpful to children who are visual learners.

Word Searches. Use graph paper or draw your own lines on regular paper to make a grid. Go through the grid and randomly write spelling words going horizontally or vertically. Fill in the rest of the spaces with any letters. Let your child go through and circle all of the spelling words they can find. Make sure you give your child a word bank to use.

All in One. When your child begins working with longer words, toward the end of first grade, you can look for smaller words inside the longer ones. Write the words on pieces of paper and cut the letters apart. Have your child see how many words they can make out of the letters. (For example, if the spelling word is *that,* you can make *at, hat,* and *that.*)

What Tests May Ask

Multiple-choice standardized tests can't be used to test expressive spelling ability (spelling your child comes up with on his own). Instead, tests that use machine-scored answer sheets must present a word and ask your child to choose the correct or incorrect spelling.

At this grade, tests may show a picture and a partially spelled word and ask your child to fill in the missing letter. Or tests may give a list of incorrectly spelled words with one correct choice and ask the child to choose the correct spelling. Alternatively, the test may give a list of correctly spelled words and ask your child to choose the one incorrect choice.

Practice Skill: Spelling

Directions: Choose the correct answer to the questions below.

Example:

Which word is spelled **correctly**?

Ⓐ coat

Ⓑ coate

Ⓒ coit

Ⓓ cout

Answer:

Ⓐ coat

1 Which word is spelled **correctly**?

Ⓐ kat

Ⓑ cate

Ⓒ cat

Ⓓ qat

2 Which word is spelled **correctly**?

Ⓐ rug

Ⓑ ruge

Ⓒ rog

Ⓓ rhug

3 Molly and Sue are friends. Molly is tall, and Sue is sma__. Which letters go in the blank?

Ⓐ tt

Ⓑ dd

Ⓒ ll

Ⓓ ss

4 The __ee has many pretty leaves. Which letters go in the blank?

Ⓐ ch

Ⓑ tr

Ⓒ sh

Ⓓ oo

5 The man is wearing a __t.
Which letters go in the blank?

Ⓐ ca

Ⓑ ba

Ⓒ ha

Ⓓ ra

6 Choose the word that is spelled **correctly.**

Ⓐ apul

Ⓑ apple

Ⓒ apel

Ⓓ uppl

7 Choose the word that is spelled **correctly.**

Ⓐ sno

Ⓑ snowe

Ⓒ snoe

Ⓓ snow

8 Choose the word that is spelled **correctly.**

Ⓐ flur

Ⓑ floor

Ⓒ flir

Ⓓ floore

9 Choose the word that is spelled **correctly.**

Ⓐ blu

Ⓑ bloo

Ⓒ bliu

Ⓓ blue

10 Choose the word that is spelled **incorrectly.**

Ⓐ hen

Ⓑ door

Ⓒ church

Ⓓ caot

11 Choose the word that is spelled **incorrectly.**

Ⓐ pigg

Ⓑ cot

Ⓒ fence

Ⓓ boy

(See page 87 for answer key.)

CHAPTER 8

Language Mechanics

In first grade, your child will learn the basic skills of language mechanics (also known as grammar). Although language mechanics instruction gets covered more completely in later grades, you can expect your child's first-grade teacher to cover capitalization, punctuation, and proper word usage.

Grammar

What First Graders Should Know

A child beginning first grade should be able to understand and speak proper English, although this may not carry over into her writing yet. In fact, your child may not even start to understand how to use language mechanics properly in her writing until the end of first grade.

In the beginning of first grade your child should know that her spoken language needs a subject and an action. She may only understand simple sentences, such as "I run" and may not have been exposed to terms like *noun* and *verb*. During her first-grade year, your child should begin to recognize nouns as *people, place, and thing words* and verbs as *doing* or *action words*. She should begin using them correctly in her spoken and written language. By the end of first grade your child should master the skill of writing and speaking using simple sentences, and she should feel confident working with more complex sentences including a subject, an action, and an object.

What You and Your Child Can Do

The best way to introduce your child to proper language skills is by modeling them. The more you use proper mechanics in your speech and writing, the faster your child will pick up the skills—and the earlier you encourage good habits, the better. Many parents are still using "baby talk" with their children throughout elementary school. While research shows baby talk with very young children helps them learn language, your school-age child won't continue to benefit from communicating this way. Don't worry that you have to sound like an English professor to teach your child proper language skills. Using correct English on a regular basis will help the skills develop naturally. Encourage your friends and family members to do the same around your child.

There are many things you can do with your child to work on all aspects of word usage. Here are some suggestions to help with correct punctuation, grammar, and capitalization.

Be Gentle. Don't go overboard in criticizing your child's mistakes in grammar. However, you can point out simple rules—"Look, see how we always capitalize the first letter in a sentence?" When your child uses improper English when speaking, restating the sentence back to your child correctly is a nonthreatening way to address a mistake.

Write On. Practice really works, especially when a child is trying to learn the basics of language mechanics. Buy some fun stationery and have your child print out thank-you notes to friends and family. Or let her write a fan letter to a politician, a movie star, or a famous author. Get her a diary or—if you're raising a computer enthusiast—a software "daily journal." Handwriting isn't the point here; instead, the goal is to help your child form a habit of writing on an everyday basis.

Read. You'll probably hear this over and over, but it's really true—reading to your child on a daily basis helps in many ways, including developing her "ear" for correct usage. Hearing the way words go together in sentences will help your child get used to hearing the English language used correctly. She'll be more likely to model correct speech and grammar herself if she hears it in the books she reads or that you read to her.

Keep a Diary. Kids this age usually love keeping a diary. There are some elaborate diaries on the market with electronic protection and voice activation. Of course, a diary doesn't have to be fancy or expensive. In fact, your child can even decorate her own spiral-bound notebook. A diary doesn't have to have a lock and key. It's just a place for your child to record her thoughts and dreams. It is also a good place for her to practice punctuation. This is also a great tool to help teach your child how to edit her own writing.

Online Writing Practice. First graders love computers, and many schools introduce them to students at this age. For those children who find it tiring to print long paragraphs with many sentences may happily peck away at a computer. Composing with a computer is also a good way for children to practice punctuation.

"Teacher for a Day." If your child finds it difficult or frustrating to produce her own writing with proper punctuation, how about letting her correct yours? Print a few paragraphs with lots of mistakes. Give her a red pencil or pen, and let her circle all the mistakes she can find. If she enjoys competition, set a timer—or give two children the same sample, and let them see who can find the most mistakes. Tell them what to watch out for and watch how much fun they have "correcting" you!

Sentence Cut-up. Write down sentences on pieces of paper and then cut them up and put them in envelopes or Ziploc bags. Have your child practice putting the sentences back together correctly. Your child will have to find the word that begins with a capital letter and the word that has punctuation at the end. These will help your child unscramble the sentence so that it looks and sounds right.

Edit on the Computer. Many first graders love to work on the computer. If your child has access to a computer and seems to enjoy it, try this activity: Write a paragraph or two, and make it funny. Include lots of word-usage errors, and then let your child edit the paragraph on the computer.

Grammar Checking Can Be Fun. If your child is fascinated by the computer, type a few paragraphs and put in plenty of punctuation mistakes. But instead of having her edit the paragraph herself, let her run your computer's "grammar check." Many kids are just fascinated by this technology! The grammar check will stop at and highlight every error, letting your child see all the mistakes. She then has the option to let the computer make its suggested correction. You can also let your child use the grammar check for her own stories she composes on the computer.

Play Computer Games. There are many terrific software games that teach language mechanics, including punctuation. Some of these games include *Reading Blaster First Grade* (Davidson), *Fair Voyage* (Arrow Educational), and *Read, Write and Type* (The Learning Company).

Capitalization

Most first graders begin school confidently printing using capital letters. Some may be vaguely aware that lowercase letters exist, but very few will actively use lowercase and capital letters correctly until their teachers insist they do so.

What First Graders Should Know

By the end of first grade, students should be able to recognize and print all letters in both uppercase and lowercase. In addition, students should understand some basic capitalization rules—for example, the first letter in the sentence is capitalized as is the first letter of a proper noun.

What Tests May Ask

Most standardized tests for first grade will assess capitalization, but most won't have the technology to have the child generate her own capitalization. Instead, the tests must rely on a child's ability to *recognize* correct capitalization rather than produce it. As a result, standardized tests today ask fairly straightforward questions about capitalization, giving a sentence and asking students to pick which word should be capitalized.

Although some computer-assisted tests are now being developed that will allow children to enter their responses into a computer to assess *expressive* capitalization skills, these aren't widely available now.

Practice Skill: Capitalization

Directions: Read these sentences. Then choose the word that should begin with a capital letter.

Example:

I live in a house in maine.

Ⓐ I

Ⓑ live

Ⓒ house

Ⓓ maine

Answer:

Ⓓ maine

1 juan is a new boy in our class.

Ⓐ juan

Ⓑ new

Ⓒ boy

Ⓓ class

2 Francesca comes to school every tuesday.

Ⓐ comes

Ⓑ school

Ⓒ every

Ⓓ tuesday

3 John gave kara a book today.

Ⓐ gave

Ⓑ kara

Ⓒ book

Ⓓ today

4 I live on river Road at the end of town.

- (A) live
- (B) river
- (C) end
- (D) town

Directions: Choose the sentence that shows correct capitalization.

Example:

- (A) Tim is Going to town today.
- (B) I love Chocolate pudding.
- (C) In March, we go to Paris.
- (D) where are you going?

Answer:

- (C) In March, we go to Paris.

5 (A) Jorge took his dog to town.
- (B) i want to go home.
- (C) My birthday is in october.
- (D) what day is it?

6 (A) Let's read a Book.
- (B) Pat and jim went to town.
- (C) Today is Sunday, March 2.
- (D) My dog's name is sandy.

(See page 87 for answer key.)

Punctuation

The first punctuation mark that your child will learn is the period that marks the end of a sentence. First-grade teachers don't usually stress punctuation at the beginning of first grade because they are more concerned with helping children get used to expressing their ideas in written form. Stressing proper punctuation doesn't occur until the second half of the school year. However, teachers do model correct punctuation when writing on charts, the board, and so on. There will be a few questions on punctuation in most standardized tests even in first grade.

What First Graders Should Know

Early first graders won't use any punctuation in their writing. It is very common in first grade for children to write stories and reports in one long sentence or paragraph, not distinguishing where one idea stops and another begins. Many first graders also read the same way, as if the copy were all one big run-on sentence, with no pauses for breaths.

By the middle of first grade, your child should have been introduced to periods, question marks, commas, and exclamation marks. At this age, most children understand the concept of sentences and the fact that they have a beginning and an ending.

What Tests May Ask

Standardized tests for first graders will focus on only very simple examples of punctuation, presenting four sentences and asking your child to choose the one that is punctuated correctly. For example, the test may present four examples of one sentence and ask which one has the period in the correct place.

Practice Skill: Punctuation

Directions: Read each question and choose the correct answer.

Example:

Which of these sentences is punctuated correctly?

- Ⓐ Jamal rode his. bike to the park.
- Ⓑ Jamal. rode his bike to the park.
- Ⓒ Jamal rode his bike to the park.
- Ⓓ Jamal rode his bike to the. park.

Answer:

- Ⓒ Jamal rode his bike to the park.

---

7 Which sentence is punctuated correctly?

- Ⓐ Harry, let's go. to the store
- Ⓑ Harry, let's go. to the store?
- Ⓒ Harry, let's go to the store.
- Ⓓ Harry, let's. go to the store.

---

8 Which sentence has the comma in the right place?

- Ⓐ Sue are you coming to the movies?
- Ⓑ Sue, are you coming to the movies?
- Ⓒ Sue are, you coming to the movies?
- Ⓓ Sue are you coming to the, movies?

---

9 Which of these sentences is punctuated correctly?

- Ⓐ Don can ride a bike?
- Ⓑ Jill, are you coming to the store.
- Ⓒ Sharon, will you bring your cup to the table?
- Ⓓ I've never been so scared in my life.

(See page 87 for answer key.)

Word Usage

It's no simple task to learn how to use the correct form of a word. Even adults often make mistakes with certain pronouns ("between you and I" instead of "between you and me"). If you knock on the door and someone calls out "Who is it?" most American adults, will answer "It's me" instead of the correct "It's I." So don't be surprised if your child has some problems in learning the correct use of some words too.

What First Graders Should Know

You can expect that your child can use correct verb tenses (present versus past), plurals, and superlatives (*small, smaller, smallest*) by the end of first grade. She may have more problems with some of the irregular forms, such as plurals of words like *goose* or *deer*.

Most first graders have a fairly good grasp of verbs and nouns, although they may not know those terms. (Some teachers refer to verbs as *doing* or *action words*.) Pronouns are more difficult for a first grader to understand. Most first graders know that *he* refers to a boy and *she* refers to a girl, but in their own writing, they may really struggle over pronouns. Your child should be able to write sentences using adjectives toward the end of the school year. Most teachers will refer to adjectives as *describing words*. A teacher may encourage this skill by helping a child change a sentence like "I have a cat." to "I have a *skinny, brown* cat." A first grader preparing for second grade should be beginning to add details to her simple-sentence writing. Children whose speech is immature ("Me want to go to bed!") or whose parents use baby talk will have an especially rough time with these skills.

What Tests May Ask

You can expect most standardized tests in first grade to assess how well your child understands word usage by presenting simple sentences and asking students to fill in the blanks with the correct form of verb, superlative, number, or pronoun.

Practice Skill: Word Usage

Directions: Read each sentence and choose the correct word to fill in the blank.

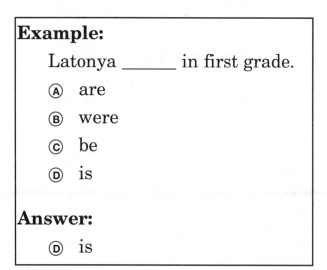

Example:

Latonya _____ in first grade.

ⓐ are

ⓑ were

ⓒ be

ⓓ is

Answer:

ⓓ is

10 Where _____ you yesterday?

ⓐ is

ⓑ were

ⓒ are

ⓓ was

11 _____ you flown on a plane before?

ⓐ Have

ⓑ Are

ⓒ Were

ⓓ Was

12 My rabbit John is _____ than Kate's rabbit.

ⓐ big

ⓑ bigger

ⓒ biggest

ⓓ bigged

13 Yesterday Dan saw one man. Today he saw two _____.

ⓐ man

ⓑ men

ⓒ mans

ⓓ mens

Directions: Read each sentence. Choose the correct pronoun for the underlined words.

Example:

Evan and Charmay like to swim.

- (A) Us
- (B) Them
- (C) They
- (D) We

Answer:

- (C) They

14 I like to play with Beth.

- (A) her
- (B) him
- (C) us
- (D) them

15 Will you give it to Jim and me?

- (A) them
- (B) ours
- (C) us
- (D) we

(See page 87 for answer key.)

CHAPTER 9

Reading Comprehension

Your child may be very good at decoding and reading individual words, but understanding those same words in context is a different thing all together. Understanding what is read is a very important skill that is introduced in first grade. This skill is commonly referred to as *reading comprehension.*

Reading comprehension is not as simple as it sounds. It's a higher-order skill that may not develop to a great degree for many children until at least second grade.

Learning how to recognize words in context, and make inferences are skills that are mastered individually at first. Eventually, a child will learn to put all these concepts together to develop good reading comprehension skills. This is why many schools understand that reading comprehension is just introduced in first grade, and they don't expect students to master the skill by the end of first grade.

You can help your child develop good reading comprehension skills by working on word recognition. The more words your child recognizes the less time he has to spend stopping to decode words as he reads. This helps the flow of the text and allows your child to make sense of what the sentences say rather than being confused by all of the stopping and starting.

What First Graders Should Know

By the time your child reaches first grade, you can expect that he will be able to make educated guesses about what will happen in a story (this is also called *predicting*). He will be able to infer meaning and anticipate events in a story as you read to him. This is the basis for reading comprehension. Your child should be able to follow a basic story line, understand the facts as they occur, and use his knowledge of that information to make predictions about what will happen next. He also should be able to answer simple questions about a story after it's read.

What You and Your Child Can Do

Read! Reading to your child is the best way to boost just about every reading-related skill, and it certainly can help reading comprehension. Reading to your child can help improve all types of reading comprehension, including listening comprehension, picture comprehension, sentence comprehension, and story comprehension.

Read Magazines. Subscribe to age-appropriate magazines such as *Stone Soup, Children's Playmate, Click, Child Life, Humpty Dumpty, Jack and Jill, Ladybug, Sesame Street Magazine, Spider, Turtle, Highlights,* or *Your Big Backyard.*

Read Newspapers. Encourage your child to read the children's page in your local newspaper, and give him the "who what where when" quiz. Point out short articles in the section that you think would interest him. If he has trouble reading the articles, help him. After he's finished, get a notebook and ask him the "who what where when" of the article. See how many he can name!

Retell Stories. This activity is a good way to get your child to think about how the story might change if it were told from another perspective. This activity works very well for tales with a strong moral, such as *The Three Little Pigs.* After you finish reading the story with your child, ask him how the story might be different if it were told not from the pigs' perspective but from the wolf's point of view.

Help Your Child. You can boost your child's comprehension by encouraging him to make predictions as he reads and to compare and contrast stories, characters, and settings; talk to him about causes and effects, help him infer meaning; and expand his vocabulary. As you read, stop and ask him what has happened. For example, if you read a story about two children who find a box buried in their backyard, you can stop and say: "Do you think there's a treasure in that box?" To answer will require your child to infer something based on the facts given so far. "No? Well, what *do* you think is in the box?" This question will require him to make a prediction about what might happen next.

Have Your Child Read. Encourage your child to read to you. By the end of the first grade, he should be able to read simple stories to you that he likes. Your child may like reading stories to you that you used to read to him when he was younger. These stories are often quite simple, but they offer big rewards for your child!

Read Mysteries and Adventures. While books such as the *Nancy Drew* or *Hardy Boys* series, or *Tom Sawyer,* may well be too difficult for a first grader to read himself, they aren't too hard for you to read *to* him. Mysteries and adventure series offer very good opportunities for your child to practice predicting what will happen next.

Listening Comprehension

The first step in developing reading comprehension is to learn how to follow a story line—and that's where listening comprehension comes in. If you've been reading to your child all along, he's gotten plenty of practice in listening carefully and remembering what he has heard. As your child gets older, he'll come to appreciate the story line and he'll be able to make predictions.

If you sit in to observe your child's class, you'll probably see the teacher read out loud to the class—and as she does so, she'll pause every so often to ask the students what they think might happen next. The teacher is working on their listening skills and predicting ability. Your child's teacher also may ask simple questions about the story as she reads to make sure the students can follow the story that is being read aloud.

What Tests May Ask

Listening skills are an important part of many standardized tests in the first grade. The tests may provide part of a story and then ask your child to predict what might happen next. Some tests have the teacher read the story out loud and have the children answer questions and make predictions based on what they heard.

Practice Skill: Listening Comprehension

Directions: Parent says to child: "I am going to read you a part of the story. Then choose what you think might happen next."

Parent reads:

Four of Jimmy's friends came to the door with presents. They all gathered around a cake.

Jimmy blew out the candles. Then they all sang a song.

---

1 What song did the children sing?

Ⓐ "Row, Row, Row Your Boat"

Ⓑ "Happy Birthday to You"

Ⓒ "I'm a Little Teapot"

Ⓓ "The Itsy Bitsy Spider"

Parent reads:

Jermaine had looked everywhere for his new puppy. Where could he be? He wasn't in the kitchen eating his food. He wasn't outdoors playing in the yard. Suddenly Jermaine smiled. He ran to the living room and looked on the cushion on the floor by the fireplace. Then he laughed.

---

2 What did Jermaine find on the cushion?

Ⓐ his cat Sparkle

Ⓑ a ball

Ⓒ a doll

Ⓓ his new puppy

(See page 88 for answer key.)

Picture Comprehension

Using picture clues when reading is the first step to your child learning to read independently. The ability to look at a picture and draw inferences from the clues it contains is an important reading comprehension skill. The ability to make predictions based on pictures in the story will help your child understand what is going on in the text. The pictures may help him correctly decode words on the page.

For example, if your child gets to an unknown word that begins with "b" and there is an illustration of a bird on the page, he may read the word *bird* based on the picture clue. Encourage your child to look at the pictures on each page before reading, because they can tell a lot about the story. This can help build confidence when reading.

What Tests May Ask

Standardized tests in first grade measure picture comprehension by presenting a picture and asking the child to answer a question based on that picture. The child will need to study the picture and find clues that he can use to answer the question.

Practice Skill: Picture Comprehension

Directions: Look at the picture and answer the question that follows it.

Example:

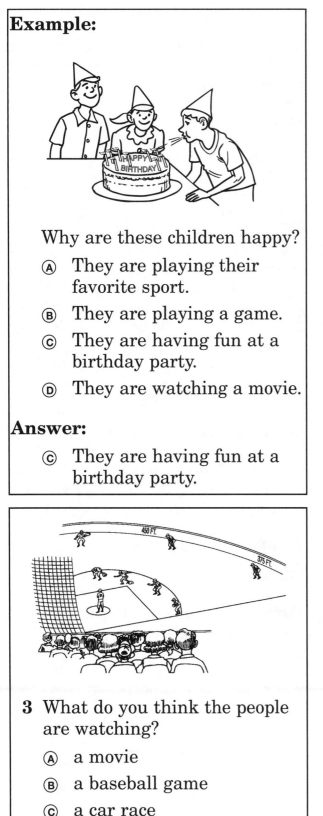

Why are these children happy?

Ⓐ They are playing their favorite sport.

Ⓑ They are playing a game.

Ⓒ They are having fun at a birthday party.

Ⓓ They are watching a movie.

Answer:

Ⓒ They are having fun at a birthday party.

3 What do you think the people are watching?

Ⓐ a movie

Ⓑ a baseball game

Ⓒ a car race

Ⓓ a pet show

4 Why is this child sad?

Ⓐ He misses his mother.

Ⓑ He lost his favorite toy.

Ⓒ His brother teased him.

Ⓓ He broke a lamp.

(See page 88 for answer key.)

Sentence Comprehension

Beginning first graders are still struggling with letter sounds and word recognition, so they are going to find sentence comprehension to be a real challenge. First graders should feel comfortable with short, simple sentences that use basic sight words in easily understandable ways. By the end of first grade, readers should begin to comprehend more complex sentences that require some amount of abstract reasoning.

What Tests May Ask

Typical standardized tests in first grade will present a sentence and then ask students to answer a question about the sentence—either choosing a word or picture that goes with the sentence.

Practice Skill: Sentence Comprehension

Directions: Read each sentence below. Decide which word or picture goes with the sentence.

Example:

If you fall down and cut your knee, use one of these.

Ⓐ pillow

Ⓑ drink

Ⓒ bandage

Ⓓ bed

Answer:

Ⓒ bandage

5 If you want to go for a ride, use this.

Ⓐ cup

Ⓑ dog

Ⓒ bed

Ⓓ car

6 If you are glad to see your grandmother, do this.

Ⓐ cry

Ⓑ hug her

Ⓒ hit her

Ⓓ run away

7 Joe is playing with Jim.

Ⓐ

Ⓑ

Ⓒ

Ⓓ

(See page 88 for answer key.)

Story Comprehension

First graders just learning to read may have trouble comprehending an entire story. They typically understand only very basic, simple stories. Even by the end of first grade when they can understand much more complex words, they still may not always gather the meaning of a whole story that they have read themselves.

A first grader may need to stop after a few pages to retell what has happened to continue following the story. Waiting until the very end to discuss the story may leave the reader confused. Your child's teacher may constantly prompt her students by asking questions about the characters or the beginning, middle, or end of the story. Your child will need a lot of prompting and practice until the skills come naturally when reading alone.

What Tests May Ask

Standardized tests for first graders may include some pictures to help in decoding stories when assessing story comprehension, but students will also need to read the story closely in order to answer the questions.

Practice Skill: Story Comprehension

Directions: Read the story and then answer the questions.

My name is Sparkle. I like to play with this ball of yarn. I like to catch mice. My girl Sandy likes to pet me. I like to climb trees. I meow when I am hungry.

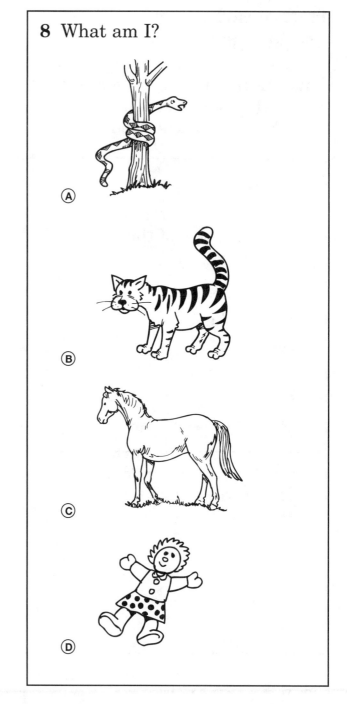

8 What am I?

Ⓐ

Ⓑ

Ⓒ

Ⓓ

David has a new baby brother. Mom and Dad just came home from the hospital. They are carrying a bundle of blankets. "Look!" they tell David. "Give this rattle to Billy."

9 Who is Billy?

Ⓐ David's puppy

Ⓑ David's grandfather

Ⓒ David's new baby brother

Ⓓ David's mother

10 What did David's parents ask David to give Billy?

Ⓐ a ball

Ⓑ a blanket

Ⓒ a rattle

Ⓓ a bottle

11 What was in the blankets?

Ⓐ a cake

Ⓑ a new puppy

Ⓒ old clothes

Ⓓ a baby

(See page 88 for answer key.

Web Sites and Resources for More Information

Homework

Homework Central
http://www.HomeworkCentral.com
Terrific site for students, parents, and teachers, filled with information, projects, and more.

Win the Homework Wars
(Sylvan Learning Centers)
http://www.educate.com/online/qa_peters.html

Reading and Grammar Help

Born to Read: How to Raise a Reader
http://www.ala.org/alsc/raise_a_reader.html

Guide to Grammar and Writing
http://webster.commnet.edu/hp/pages/darling/grammar.htm
Help with "plague words and phrases," grammar FAQs, sentence parts, punctuation, rules for common usage.

Internet Public Library: Reading Zone
http://www.ipl.org/cgi-bin/youth/youth.out

Keeping Kids Reading and Writing
http://www.tiac.net/users/maryl/

U.S. Dept. of Education: Helping Your Child Learn to Read
http://www.ed.gov/pubs/parents/Reading/index.html

Math Help

Center for Advancement of Learning
http://www.muskingum.edu/%7Ecal/database/Math2.html
Substitution and memory strategies for math.

Center for Advancement of Learning
http://www.muskingum.edu/%7Ecal/database/Math1.html
General tips and suggestions.

Math.com
http://www.math.com
The world of math online.

Math.com
http://www.math.com/student/testprep.html
Get ready for standardized tests.

Math.com: Homework Help in Math
http://www.math.com/students/homework.html

Math.com: Math for Homeschoolers
http://www.math.com/parents/homeschool.html

The Math Forum: Problems and Puzzles
http://forum.swarthmore.edu/library/resource_types/problems_puzzles
Lots of fun math puzzles and problems for grades K through 12.

The Math Forum: Math Tips and Tricks
http://forum.swarthmore.edu/k12/mathtips/mathtips.html

Tips on Testing

Books on Test Preparation
http://www.testbooksonline.com/preHS.asp
This site provides printed resources for parents who wish to help their children prepare for standardized school tests.

Core Knowledge Web Site
http://www.coreknowledge.org/
Site dedicated to providing resources for parents; based on the books of E. D. Hirsch, Jr., who wrote the *What Your X Grader Needs to Know* series.

Family Education Network
http://www.familyeducation.com/article/0,1120, 1-6219,00.html
This report presents some of the arguments against current standardized testing practices in the public schools. The site also provides links to family activities that help kids learn.

Math.com
http://www.math.com/students/testprep.html
Get ready for standardized tests.

Standardized Tests
http://arc.missouri.edu/k12/
K through 12 assessment tools and know-how.

Parents: Testing in Schools

KidSource: Talking to Your Child's Teacher about Standardized Tests
http://www.kidsource.com/kidsource/content2/ talking.assessment.k12.4.html
This site provides basic information to help parents understand their children's test results and provides pointers for how to discuss the results with their children's teachers.

eSCORE.com: State Test and Education Standards
http://www.eSCORE.com
Find out if your child meets the necessary requirements for your local schools. A Web site with experts from Brazelton Institute and Harvard's Project Zero.

Overview of States' Assessment Programs
http://ericae.net/faqs/

Parent Soup
Education Central: Standardized Tests
http://www.parentsoup.com/edcentral/testing
A parent's guide to standardized testing in the schools, written from a parent advocacy standpoint.

National Center for Fair and Open Testing, Inc. (FairTest)
342 Broadway
Cambridge, MA 02139
(617) 864-4810
http://www.fairtest.org

National Parent Information Network
http://npin.org

Publications for Parents from the U.S. Department of Education
http://www.ed.gov/pubs/parents/
An ever-changing list of information for parents available from the U.S. Department of Education.

State of the States Report
http://www.edweek.org/sreports/qc99/states/ indicators/in-intro.htm
A report on testing and achievement in the 50 states.

Testing: General Information

Academic Center for Excellence
http://www.acekids.com

American Association for Higher Education Assessment
http://www.aahe.org/assessment/web.htm

American Educational Research Association (AERA)
http://aera.net
An excellent link to reports on American education, including reports on the controversy over standardized testing.

American Federation of Teachers
555 New Jersey Avenue, NW
Washington, D.C. 20011

Association of Test Publishers Member Products and Services
http://www.testpublishers.org/memserv.htm

Education Week on the Web
http://www.edweek.org

ERIC Clearinghouse on Assessment and Evaluation
1131 Shriver Lab
University of Maryland
College Park, MD 20742
http://ericae.net
A clearinghouse of information on assessment and education reform.

FairTest: The National Center for Fair and Open Testing
http://fairtest.org/facts/ntfact.htm
http://fairtest.org/
The National Center for Fair and Open Testing is an advocacy organization working to end the abuses, misuses, and flaws of standardized testing and to ensure that evaluation of students and workers is fair, open, and educationally sound. This site provides many links to fact sheets, opinion papers, and other sources of information about testing.

National Congress of Parents and Teachers
700 North Rush Street
Chicago, Illinois 60611

National Education Association
1201 16th Street, NW
Washington, DC 20036

National School Boards Association
http://www.nsba.org
A good source for information on all aspects of public education, including standardized testing.

Testing Our Children: A Report Card on State Assessment Systems
http://www.fairtest.org/states/survey.htm
Report of testing practices of the states, with graphical links to the states and a critique of fair testing practices in each state.

Trends in Statewide Student Assessment Programs: A Graphical Summary
http://www.ccsso.org/survey96.html
Results of annual survey of states' departments of public instruction regarding their testing practices.

U.S. Department of Education
http://www.ed.gov/

Web Links for Parents Who Want to Help Their Children Achieve
http://www.liveandlearn.com/learn.html
This page offers many Web links to free and for-sale information and materials for parents who want to help their children do well in school. Titles include such free offerings as the Online Colors Game and questionnaires to determine whether your child is ready for school.

What Should Parents Know about Standardized Testing in the Schools?
http://www.rusd.k12.ca.us/parents/standard.html
An online brochure about standardized testing in the schools, with advice regarding how to become an effective advocate for your child.

Test Publishers Online

ACT: Information for Life's Transitions
http://www.act.org

American Guidance Service, Inc.
http://www.agsnet.com

Ballard & Tighe Publishers
http://www.ballard-tighe.com

Consulting Psychologists Press
http://www.cpp-db.com

CTB McGraw-Hill
http://www.ctb.com

Educational Records Bureau
http://www.erbtest.org/index.html

Educational Testing Service
http://www.ets.org

General Educational Development (GED) Testing Service

http://www.acenet.edu/calec/ged/home.html

Harcourt Brace Educational Measurement

http://www.hbem.com

Piney Mountain Press—A Cyber-Center for Career and Applied Learning

http://www.pineymountain.com

ProEd Publishing

http://www.proedinc.com

Riverside Publishing Company

http://www.hmco.com/hmco/riverside

Stoelting Co.

http://www.stoeltingco.com

Sylvan Learning Systems, Inc.

http://www.educate.com

Touchstone Applied Science Associates, Inc. (TASA)

http://www.tasa.com

Tests Online

(*Note:* We don't endorse tests; some may not have technical documentation. Evaluate the quality of any testing program before making decisions based on its use.)

Edutest, Inc.

http://www.edutest.com

Edutest is an Internet-accessible testing service that offers criterion-referenced tests for elementary school students, based upon the standards for K through 12 learning and achievement in the states of Virginia, California, and Florida.

Virtual Knowledge

http://www.smarterkids.com

This commercial service, which enjoys a formal partnership with Sylvan Learning Centers, offers a line of skills assessments for preschool through grade 9 for use in the classroom or the home. For free online sample tests, see the Virtual Test Center.

Read More about It

Abbamont, Gary W. *Test Smart: Ready-to-Use Test-Taking Strategies and Activities for Grades 5–12*. Upper Saddle River, NJ: Prentice Hall Direct, 1997.

Cookson, Peter W., and Joshua Halberstam. *A Parent's Guide to Standardized Tests in School: How to Improve Your Child's Chances for Success*. New York: Learning Express, 1998.

Frank, Steven, and Stephen Frank. *Test-Taking Secrets: Study Better, Test Smarter, and Get Great Grades (The Backpack Study Series)*. Holbrook, MA: Adams Media Corporation, 1998.

Gilbert, Sara Dulaney. *How to Do Your Best on Tests: A Survival Guide*. New York: Beech Tree Books, 1998.

Gruber, Gary. *Dr. Gary Gruber's Essential Guide to Test-Taking for Kids, Grades 3–5*. New York: William Morrow & Co., 1986.

———. *Gary Gruber's Essential Guide to Test-Taking for Kids, Grades 6, 7, 8, 9*. New York: William Morrow & Co., 1997.

Leonhardt, Mary. *99 Ways to Get Kids to Love Reading and 100 Books They'll Love*. New York: Crown, 1997.

———. *Parents Who Love Reading, Kids Who Don't: How It Happens and What You Can Do about It*. New York: Crown, 1995.

McGrath, Barbara B. *The Baseball Counting Book*. Watertown, MA: Charlesbridge, 1999.

———. *More M&M's Brand Chocolate Candies Math*. Watertown, MA: Charlesbridge, 1998.

Mokros, Janice R. *Beyond Facts & Flashcards: Exploring Math with Your Kids*. Portsmouth, NH: Heinemann, 1996.

Romain, Trevor, and Elizabeth Verdick. *True or False?: Tests Stink!* Minneapolis: Free Spirit Publishing Co., 1999.

Schartz, Eugene M. *How to Double Your Child's Grades in School: Build Brilliance and Leadership into Your Child—from Kindergarten to College—in Just 5 Minutes a Day*. New York: Barnes & Noble, 1999.

Taylor, Kathe, and Sherry Walton. *Children at the Center: A Workshop Approach to Standardized Test Preparation, K–8*. Portsmouth, NH: Heinemann, 1998.

Tobia, Sheila. *Overcoming Math Anxiety*. New York: W. W. Norton & Company, Inc., 1995.

Tufariello, Ann Hunt. *Up Your Grades: Proven Strategies for Academic Success*. Lincolnwood, IL: VGM Career Horizons, 1996.

Vorderman, Carol. *How Math Works*. Pleasantville, NY: Reader's Digest Association, Inc., 1996.

Zahler, Kathy A. *50 Simple Things You Can Do to Raise a Child Who Loves to Read*. New York: IDG Books, 1997.

What Your Child's Test Scores Mean

Several weeks or months after your child has taken standardized tests, you will receive a report such as the TerraNova Home Report found in Figures 1 and 2. You will receive similar reports if your child has taken other tests. We briefly examine what information the reports include.

Look at the first page of the Home Report. Note that the chart provides labeled bars showing the child's performance. Each bar is labeled with the child's National Percentile for that skill area. When you know how to interpret them, national percentiles can be the most useful scores you encounter on reports such as this. Even when you are confronted with different tests that use different scale scores, you can always interpret percentiles the same way, regardless of the test. A percentile tells the percent of students who score at or below that level. A percentile of 25, for example, means that 25 percent of children taking the test scored at or below that score. (It also means that 75 percent of students scored above that score.) Note that the average is always at the 50th percentile.

On the right side of the graph on the first page of the report, the publisher has designated the ranges of scores that constitute average, above average, and below average. You can also use this slightly more precise key for interpreting percentiles:

PERCENTILE RANGE	LEVEL
2 and Below	Deficient
3–8	Borderline
9–23	Low Average
24–75	Average
76–97	High Average
98 and Up	Superior

The second page of the Home report provides a listing of the child's strengths and weaknesses, along with keys for mastery, partial mastery, and non-mastery of the skills. Scoring services determine these breakdowns based on the child's scores as compared with those from the national norm group.

Your child's teacher or guidance counselor will probably also receive a profile report similar to the TerraNova Individual Profile Report, shown in Figures 3 and 4. That report will be kept in your child's permanent record. The first aspect of this report to notice is that the scores are expressed both numerically and graphically.

First look at the score bands under National Percentile. Note that the scores are expressed as bands, with the actual score represented by a dot within each band. The reason we express the scores as bands is to provide an idea of the amount by which typical scores may vary for each student. That is, each band represents a

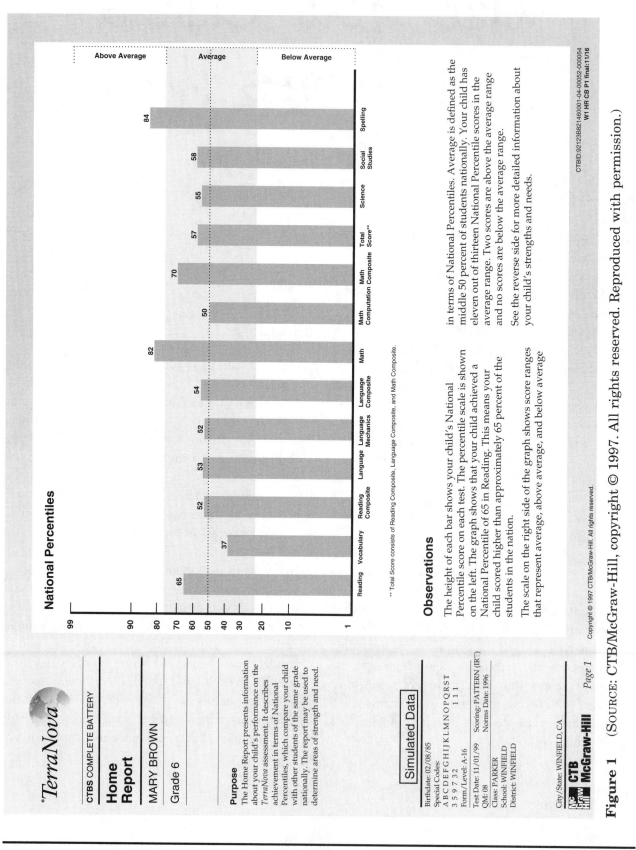

Figure 1 (SOURCE: CTB/McGraw-Hill, copyright © 1997. All rights reserved. Reproduced with permission.)

TerraNova

CTBS COMPLETE BATTERY

Home Report

MARY BROWN

Grade 6

Purpose

This page of the Home Report presents information about your child's strengths and needs. This information is provided to help you monitor your child's academic growth.

Simulated Data

Birthdate: 02/08/85
Special Codes:
A B C D E F G H I J K L M N O P Q R S T
3 5 9 7 3 2   1 1 1
Test Date: 11/01/99   Scoring: PATTERN (IRT)
QM: 08   Norms Date: 1996

Class: PARKER
School: WINFIELD
District: WINFIELD

City/State: WINFIELD, CA

Strengths

Reading
● Basic Understanding
● Analyze Text

Vocabulary
● Word Meaning
● Words in Context

Language
● Editing Skills
● Sentence Structure

Language Mechanics
● Sentences, Phrases, Clauses

Mathematics
● Computation and Numerical Estimation
● Operation Concepts

Mathematics Computation
● Add Whole Numbers
● Multiply Whole Numbers

Science
● Life Science
● Inquiry Skills

Social Studies
● Geographic Perspectives
● Economic Perspectives

Spelling
● Vowels
● Consonants

Key ● **Mastery**

Needs

Reading
◐ Evaluate and Extend Meaning
○ Identify Reading Strategies

Vocabulary
○ Multimeaning Words

Language
◐ Writing Strategies

Language Mechanics
○ Writing Conventions

Mathematics
◐ Measurement
◐ Geometry and Spatial Sense

Mathematics Computation
○ Percents

Science
○ Earth and Space Science

Social Studies
◐ Historical and Cultural Perspectives

Spelling
No area of needs were identified for this content area

Key ◐ **Partial Mastery**   ○ **Non-Mastery**

General Interpretation

The left column shows your child's best areas of performance. In each case, your child has reached mastery level. The column at the right shows the areas within each test section where your child's scores are the lowest. In these cases, your child has not reached mastery level, although he or she may have reached partial mastery.

CTBID:92123B821460001-04-00052-000054
W1 CB HR P2 Final:11/05

■ CTB
■ McGraw-Hill

Page 2

Figure 2   (SOURCE: CTB/McGraw-Hill, copyright © 1997. All rights reserved. Reproduced with permission.)

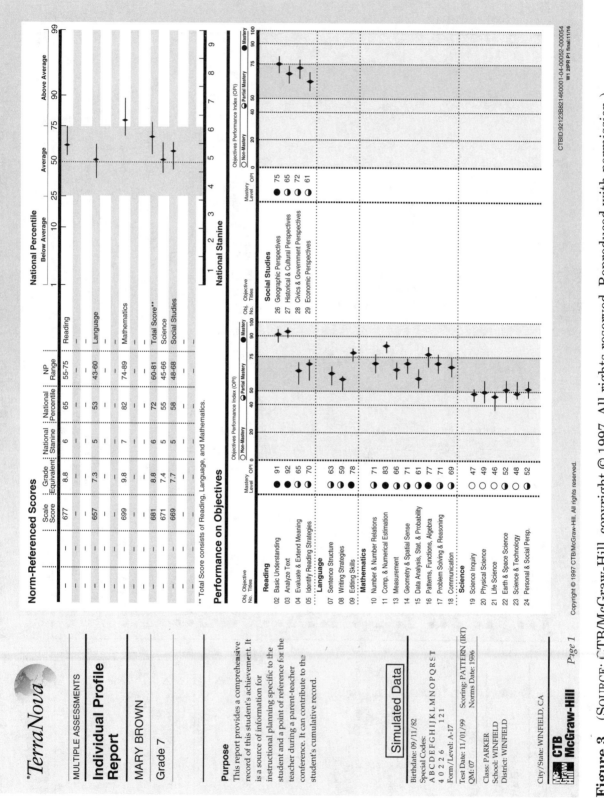

Figure 3 (SOURCE: CTB/McGraw-Hill, copyright © 1997. All rights reserved. Reproduced with permission.)

Observations

Norm-Referenced Scores

The top section of the report presents information about this student's achievement in several different ways. The National Percentile (NP) data and graph indicate how this student performed compared to students of the same grade nationally. The National Percentile range indicates that if this student had taken the test numerous times the scores would have fallen within the range shown. The shaded area on the graph represents the average range of scores, usually defined as the middle 50 percent of students nationally. Scores in the area to the right of the shading are above the average range. Scores in the area to the left of the shading are below the average range.

In Reading, for example, this student achieved a National Percentile rank of 65. This student scored higher than 65 percent of the students nationally. This score is in the average range. This student has a total of five scores in the average range. One score is in the above average range. No scores are in the below average range.

Performance on Objectives

The next section of the report presents performance on the objectives. Each objective is measured by a minimum of 4 items. The Objectives Performance Index (OPI) provides an estimate of the number of items that a student could be expected to answer correctly if there had been 100 items for that objective. The OPI is used to indicate mastery of each objective. An OPI of 75 and above characterizes Mastery. An OPI between 50 and 74 indicates Partial Mastery, and an OPI below 50 indicates Non-Mastery. The two-digit number preceding the objective title identifies the objective, which is fully described in the Teacher's Guide to *TerraNova*. The bands on either side of the diamonds indicate the range within which the student's test scores would fall if the student were tested numerous times.

In Reading, for example, this student could be expected to respond correctly to 91 out of 100 items measuring Basic Understanding. If this student had taken the test numerous times the OPI for this objective would have fallen between 82 and 93.

Teacher Notes

TerraNova

MULTIPLE ASSESSMENTS

Individual Profile Report

MARY BROWN

Grade 7

Purpose

The Observations section of the Individual Profile Report gives teachers and parents information to interpret this report. This page is a narrative description of the data on the other side.

Simulated Data

Birthdate: 09/11/82
Special Codes:
A B C D E F G H I J K L M N O P Q R S T
4 0 2 2 6   1 2 1
Form/Level: A-17

Test Date: 11/01/99   Scoring: PATTERN (IRT)
QM: 08   Norms Date: 1996

Class: PARKER
School: WINFIELD
District: WINFIELD

City/State: WINFIELD, CA

CTB
McGraw-Hill

Page 2

Figure 4 (SOURCE: CTB/McGraw-Hill, copyright © 1997. All rights reserved. Reproduced with permission.)

TerraNova

MULTIPLE ASSESSMENTS

Student Performance Level Report

KEN ALLEN

Grade 4

Purpose

This report describes this student's achievement in terms of five performance levels for each content area. The meaning of these levels is described on the back of this page. Performance levels are a new way of describing achievement.

Simulated Data

Birthdate: 02/08/86
Special Codes:
A B C D E F G H I J K L M N O P Q R S T
3 5 9 7 3 2   1 1 1
Form/Level: A-14
Test Date: 04/15/97   Scoring: PATTERN (IRT)
QM: 31   Norms Date: 1996

Class: SCHWARZ
School: WINFIELD
District: GREEN VALLEY

City/State: WINFIELD, CA

Performance Levels	Reading	Language	Mathematics	Science	Social Studies
5 Advanced					
4 Proficient	✓				
3 Nearing Proficiency	✓	✓	✓	✓	✓
2 Progressing	✓	✓	✓	✓	✓
1 Step 1	✓	✓	✓	✓	✓

Partially Proficient

Observations

Performance level scores provide a measure of what students *can do* in terms of the content and skills assessed by *TerraNova*, and typically found in curricula for Grades 3, 4, and 5. It is desirable to work towards achieving a Level 4 (Proficient) or Level 5 (Advanced) by the end of Grade 5.

The number of check marks indicates the performance level this student reached in each content area. For example, this student reached Level 3 in Reading and Social Studies.

The performance level indicates this student can perform the majority of what is described for that level and even more of what is described for the levels below. The student may also be capable of performing some of the things described in the next higher level, but not enough to have reached that level of performance.

For example, this student can perform the majority of what is described for Level 3 in Reading and even more of what is described for Level 2 and Level 1 in Reading. This student may also be capable of performing some of what is described for Level 4 in Reading.

For each content area look at the skills and knowledge described in the next higher level. These are the competencies this student needs to demonstrate to show academic growth.

CTB
McGraw-Hill

Page 1

CTBID:92123B821460001-04-00052-000054
W1 SPLR P1 final:11/09

Figure 5 (SOURCE: CTB/McGraw-Hill, copyright © 1997. All rights reserved. Reproduced with permission.)

Performance Levels (Grades 3, 4, 5)	Reading	Language	Mathematics	Science	Social Studies
5 Advanced	Students use analogies to generalize. They identify a paraphrase of concepts or ideas in texts. They can indicate thought processes that led them to a previous answer. In written responses, they demonstrate understanding of an implied theme, assess intent of passage information, and provide justification as well as support for their answers.	Students understand logical development in paragraph structure. They identify essential information from notes. They recognize the effect of prepositional phrases on subject-verb agreement. They find and correct at least 4 out of 6 errors when editing simple narratives. They correct run-on and incomplete sentences in more complex texts. They can eliminate all errors when editing their own work.	Students locate decimals on a number line; compute with decimals and fractions; read scale drawings; find areas; identify geometric transformations; construct and label bar graphs; find simple probabilities; find averages; use patterns in data to solve problems; use multiple strategies and concepts to solve unfamiliar problems; express mathematical ideas and explain the problem-solving process.	Students understand a broad range of grade level scientific concepts, such as the structure of Earth and instinctive behavior. They know terminology, such as decomposers, fossil fuel, eclipse, and buoyancy. Knowledge of more complex environmental issues includes, for example, the positive consequences of a forest fire. Students can process and interpret more detailed tables and graphs. They can suggest improvements to experimental design, such as running more trials.	Students consistently demonstrate skills such as synthesizing information from two sources (e.g., a document and a map). They show understanding of the democratic process and global environmental issues, and know the location of continents and major countries. They analyze and summarize information from multiple sources in early American history. They thoroughly explain both sides of an issue and give complete and detailed written answers to questions.
4 Proficient	Students interpret figures of speech. They recognize paraphrase of text information and retrieve information to complete forms. In more complex texts, they identify themes, main ideas, or author purpose/point of view. They analyze and apply information in graphic and text form, make reasonable generalizations, and draw conclusions. In written responses, they can identify key elements from text.	Students select the best supporting sentences for a topic sentence. They use compound predicates to combine sentences. They identify simple subjects and predicates, recognize correct usage when confronted with two types of errors, and find and correct at least 3 out of 6 errors when editing simple narratives. They can edit their own work with only minor errors.	Students compare, order, and round whole numbers; know place value to thousands; identify fractions; use computation and estimation strategies; relate multiplication to addition; measure to nearest half-inch and centimeter; measure and find perimeters; estimate measures; find elapsed times; combine and subdivide shapes; identify parallel lines; interpret tables and graphs; solve two-step problems.	Students have a range of specific science knowledge, including details about animal adaptations and classification, states of matter, and the geology of Earth. They recognize scientific words such as habitat, gravity, and mass. They understand the usefulness of computers. They understand reasons for conserving natural resources. Understanding of experimentation includes analyzing purpose, interpreting data, and selecting tools to gather data.	Students demonstrate skills such as making inferences, using historical documents and analyzing maps to determine the economic strengths of a region. They understand the function of currency in various cultures and supply and demand. They summarize information from multiple sources, recognize relationships, determine relevance of information, and show global awareness. They propose solutions to real-world problems and support ideas with appropriate details.
3 Nearing Proficiency	Students use context clues and structural analysis to determine word meaning. They recognize homonyms and antonyms in grade-level text. They identify important details, sequence, cause and effect, and lessons embedded in the text. They interpret characters' feelings and apply information to new situations. In written responses, they can express an opinion and support it.	Students identify irrelevant sentences in paragraphs and identify the best place to insert new information. They recognize faulty sentence construction. They can combine simple sentences with subordination of phrases/clauses. They identify reference sources. They recognize correct conventions for dates, closings, and place names in informal correspondence.	Students identify even and odd numbers; subtract whole numbers with regrouping; multiply and divide by one-digit numbers; identify simple fractions; measure with ruler to nearest inch; tell time to nearest fifteen minutes; recognize and classify common shapes; recognize symmetry; subdivide shapes; complete bar graphs; extend numerical and geometric patterns; apply simple logical reasoning.	Students are familiar with the life cycles of plants and animals. They can identify an example of a cold-blooded animal. They infer what once existed from fossil evidence. They recognize the term habitat. They understand the water cycle. They know science and society issues such as recycling and sources of pollution. They can sequence technological advances. They extrapolate data, devise a simple classification scheme, and determine the purpose of a simple experiment.	Students demonstrate skills in organizing information. They use time lines, product and global maps, and cardinal directions. They understand simple cause and effect relationships and historical documents. They sequence events, associate holidays with events, and classify natural resources. They compare life in different times and understand some economic concepts related to products, jobs, and the environment. They give some detail in written responses.
2 Progressing	Students identify synonyms for grade-level words, and use context clues to define common words. They make simple inferences and predictions based on text. They identify characters' feelings. They can transfer information from text to graphic form, or from graphic form to text. In written responses, they can provide limited support for their answers.	Students identify the use of correct verb tenses and supply verbs to complete sentences. They complete paragraphs by selecting an appropriate topic sentence. They select correct adjective forms.	Students know ordinal numbers; solve coin combination problems; count by tens; add whole numbers with regrouping; have basic estimation skills; understand addition property of zero; write and identify number sentences describing simple situations; read calendars; identify appropriate measurement tools; recognize congruent figures; use simple coordinate grids; read common tables and graphs.	Students recognize that plants decompose and become part of soil. They can classify a plant as a vegetable. They recognize that camouflage relates to survival. They recognize basic science terms such as hibernate. They have an understanding of human impact on the environment and are familiar with the causes of pollution. They find the correct bar graph to represent given data and transfer data appropriate for middle elementary grades to a bar graph.	Students demonstrate simple information-processing skills such as using basic maps and keys. They recognize simple geographical terms, types of jobs, modes of transportation, and natural resources. They connect a human need with an appropriate community service. They identify some early famous presidents and know the capital of the United States. Their written answers are partially complete.
1 Step 1	Students select pictured representations of ideas and identify stated details contained in simple texts. In written responses, they can select and transfer information from charts.	Students supply subjects to complete sentences. They identify the correct use of pronouns. They edit for the correct use of end marks and initial capital letters, and identify the correct convention for greetings in letters.	Students read and recognize numbers to 1000; identify real-world uses of numbers; add and subtract two-digit numbers without regrouping; identify addition situations; recognize and complete simple geometric and numerical patterns.	Students recognize basic adaptations for living in the water, identify an animal that is hatched from an egg, and associate an organism with its correct environment. They identify an object as metal. They have some understanding of conditions on the moon. They supply one way a computer can be useful. They associate an instrument like a telescope with a field of study.	Students are developing fundamental social studies skills such as locating and classifying basic information. They locate information in pictures and read and complete simple bar graphs related to social studies concepts and contexts. They can connect some city buildings with their functions and recognize certain historical objects.

Partially Proficient

W1 SPLR P2:11/02

IMPORTANT: Each performance level, depicted on the other side, indicates the student can perform the majority of what is described for that level and even more of what is described for the levels below. The student may also be capable of performing some of the things described in the next higher level, but not enough to have reached that level.

Figure 6 (Source: CTB/McGraw-Hill, copyright © 1997. All rights reserved. Reproduced with permission.)

confidence interval. In these reports, we usually report either a 90 percent or 95 percent confidence interval. Interpret a confidence interval this way: Suppose we report a 90 percent confidence interval of 25 to 37. This means we estimate that, if the child took the test multiple times, we would expect that child's score to be in the 25 to 37 range 90 percent of the time.

Now look under the section titled Norm-Referenced Scores on the first page of the Individual Profile Report (Figure 3). The farthest column on the right provides the NP Range, which is the National Percentile scores represented by the score bands in the chart.

Next notice the column labeled Grade Equivalent. Theoretically, grade level equivalents equate a student's score in a skill area with the average grade placement of children who made the same score. Many psychologists and test developers would prefer that we stopped reporting grade equivalents, because they can be grossly misleading. For example, the average reading grade level of high school seniors as reported by one of the more popular tests is the eighth grade level. Does that mean that the nation's high school seniors cannot read? No. The way the test publisher calculated grade equivalents was to determine the average test scores for students in grades 4 to 6 and then simply extend the resulting prediction formula to grades 7 to 12. The result is that parents of average high school seniors who take the test in question would mistakenly believe that their seniors are reading four grade levels behind! Stick to the percentile in interpreting your child's scores.

Now look at the columns labeled Scale Score and National Stanine. These are two of a group of scores we also call *standard scores.* In reports for other tests, you may see other standard scores reported, such as Normal Curve Equivalents (NCEs), Z-Scores, and T-Scores. The IQ that we report on intelligence tests, for example, is a standard score. Standard scores are simply a way of expressing a student's scores in terms of the statistical properties of the scores from the norm group against which we are comparing the child. Although most psychologists prefer to speak in terms of standard scores among themselves, parents are advised to stick to percentiles in interpreting your child's performance.

Now look at the section of the report labeled Performance on Objectives. In this section, the test publisher reports how your child did on the various skills that make up each skills area. Note that the scores on each objective are expressed as a percentile band, and you are again told whether your child's score constitutes mastery, non-mastery, or partial mastery. Note that these scores are made up of tallies of sometimes small numbers of test items taken from sections such as Reading or Math. Because they are calculated from a much smaller number of scores than the main scales are (for example, Sentence Comprehension is made up of fewer items than overall Reading), their scores are less reliable than those of the main scales.

Now look at the second page of the Individual Profile Report (Figure 4). Here the test publisher provides a narrative summary of how the child did on the test. These summaries are computer-generated according to rules provided by the publisher. Note that the results descriptions are more general than those on the previous three report pages. But they allow the teacher to form a general picture of which students are performing at what general skill levels.

Finally, your child's guidance counselor may receive a summary report such as the TerraNova Student Performance Level Report. (See Figures 5 and 6.) In this report, the publisher explains to school personnel what skills the test assessed and generally how proficiently the child tested under each skill.

Which States Require Which Tests

Tables 1 through 3 summarize standardized testing practices in the 50 states and the District of Columbia. This information is constantly changing; the information presented here was accurate as of the date of printing of this book. Many states have changed their testing practices in response to revised accountability legislation, while others have changed the tests they use.

Table 1   State Web Sites: Education and Testing

STATE	GENERAL WEB SITE	STATE TESTING WEB SITE
Alabama	http://www.alsde.edu/	http://www.fairtest.org/states/al.htm
Alaska	www.educ.state.ak.us/	http://www.educ.state.ak.us/
Arizona	http://www.ade.state.az.us/	http://www.ade.state.az.us/standards/
Arkansas	http://arkedu.k12.ar.us/	http://www.fairtest.org/states/ar.htm
California	http://goldmine.cde.ca.gov/	http://star.cde.ca.gov/
Colorado	http://www.cde.state.co.us/index_home.htm	http://www.cde.state.co.us/index_assess.htm
Connecticut	http://www.state.ct.us/sde/	http://www.state.ct.us/sde/cmt/index.htm
Delaware	http://www.doe.state.de.us/	http://www.doe.state.de.us/aab/index.htm
District of Columbia	http://www.k12.dc.us/dcps/home.html	http://www.k12.dc.us/dcps/data/data_frame2.html
Florida	http://www.firn.edu/doe/	http://www.firn.edu/doe/sas/sasshome.htm
Georgia	http://www.doe.k12.ga.us/	http://www.doe.k12.ga.us/sla/ret/recotest.html
Hawaii	http://kalama.doe.hawaii.edu/upena/	http://www.fairtest.org/states/hi.htm
Idaho	http://www.sde.state.id.us/Dept/	http://www.sde.state.id.us/instruct/schoolaccount/statetesting.htm
Illinois	http://www.isbe.state.il.us/	http://www.isbe.state.il.us/isat/
Indiana	http://doe.state.in.us/	http://doe.state.in.us/assessment/welcome.html
Iowa	http://www.state.ia.us/educate/index.html	(Tests Chosen Locally)
Kansas	http://www.ksbe.state.ks.us/	http://www.ksbe.state.ks.us/assessment/
Kentucky	http://www.kde.state.ky.us/	http://www.kde.state.ky.us/oaa/
Louisiana	http://www.doe.state.la.us/DOE/asps/home.asp	http://www.doe.state.la.us/DOE/asps/home.asp?I-HISTAKES
Maine	http://janus.state.me.us/education/homepage.htm	http://janus.state.me.us/education/mea/meacompass.htm
Maryland	http://www.msde.state.md.us/	http://msp.msde.state.md.us/
Massachusetts	http://www.doe.mass.edu/	http://www.doe.mass.edu/mcas/
Michigan	http://www.mde.state.mi.us/	http://www.MeritAward.state.mi.us/merit/meap/index.htm

STATE	GENERAL WEB SITE	STATE TESTING WEB SITE
Minnesota	http://www.educ.state.mn.us/	http://fairtest.org/states/mn.htm
Mississippi	http://mdek12.state.ms.us/	http://fairtest.org/states/ms.htm
Missouri	http://services.dese.state.mo.us/	http://fairtest.org/states/mo.htm
Montana	http://www.metnet.state.mt.us/	http://fairtest.org/states/mt.htm
Nebraska	http://www.nde.state.ne.us/	http://www.edneb.org/IPS/AppAccrd/ApprAccrd.html
Nevada	http://www.nde.state.nv.us/	http://www.nsn.k12.nv.us/nvdoe/reports/TerraNova.doc
New Hampshire	http://www.state.nh.us/doe/	http://www.state.nh.us/doe/Assessment/assessme(NHEIAP).htm
New Jersey	http://www.state.nj.us/education/	http://www.state.nj.us/njded/stass/index.html
New Mexico	http://sde.state.nm.us/	http://sde.state.nm.us/press/august30a.html
New York	http://www.nysed.gov/	http://www.emsc.nysed.gov/ciai/assess.html
North Carolina	http://www.dpi.state.nc.us/	http://www.dpi.state.nc.us/accountability/reporting/index.html
North Dakota	http://www.dpi.state.nd.us/dpi/index.htm	http://www.dpi.state.nd.us/dpi/reports/assess/assess.htm
Ohio	http://www.ode.state.oh.us/	http://www.ode.state.oh.us/ca/
Oklahoma	http://sde.state.ok.us/	http://sde.state.ok.us/acrob/testpack.pdf
Oregon	http://www.ode.state.or.us//	http://www.ode.state.or.us//asmt/index.htm
Pennsylvania	http://www.pde.psu.edu/	http://www.fairtest.org/states/pa.htm
Rhode Island	http://www.ridoe.net/	http://www.ridoe.net/standards/default.htm
South Carolina	http://www.state.sc.us/sde/	http://www.state.sc.us/sde/reports/terranov.htm
South Dakota	http://www.state.sd.us/state/executive/deca/	http://www.state.sd.us/state/executive/deca/TA/McRelReport/McRelReports.htm
Tennessee	http://www.state.tn.us/education/	http://www.state.tn.us/education/tsintro.htm
Texas	http://www.tea.state.tx.us/	http://www.tea.state.tx.us/student.assessment/
Utah	http://www.usoe.k12.ut.us/	http://www.usoe.k12.ut.us/eval/usoeeval.htm
Vermont	http://www.state.vt.us/educ/	http://www.fairtest.org/states/vt.htm

STATE	GENERAL WEB SITE	STATE TESTING WEB SITE
Virginia	http://www.pen.k12.va.us/Anthology/VDOE/	http://www.pen.k12.va.us/VDOE/Assessment/home.shtml
Washington	http://www.k12.wa.us/	http://www.k12.wa.us/assessment/
West Virginia	http://wvde.state.wv.us/	http://wvde.state.wv.us/
Wisconsin	http://www.dpi.state.wi.us/	http://www.dpi.state.wi.us/dpi/dltcl/eis/achfacts.html
Wyoming	http://www.k12.wy.us/wdehome.html	http://www.asme.com/wycas/index.htm

Table 2 Norm-Referenced and Criterion-Referenced Tests Administered by State

STATE	NORM-REFERENCED TEST	CRITERION-REFERENCED TEST	EXIT EXAM
Alabama	Stanford Achievement Test		Alabama High School Graduation Exam
Alaska	California Achievement Test	Alaska Benchmark Examinations	
Arizona	Stanford Achievement Test	Arizona's Instrument to Measure Standards (AIMS)	
Arkansas	Stanford Achievement Test		
California	Stanford Achievement Test	Standardized Testing and Reporting Supplement	High School Exit Exam (HSEE)
Colorado	None	Colorado Student Assessment Program	
Connecticut		Connecticut Mastery Test	
Delaware	Stanford Achievement Test	Delaware Student Testing Program	
District of Columbia	Stanford Achievement Test		
Florida	(Locally Selected)	Florida Comprehensive Assessment Test (FCAT)	High School Competency Test (HSCT)
Georgia	Stanford Achievement Test	Georgia Kindergarten Assessment Program—Revised and Criterion-Referenced Competency Tests (CRCT)	Georgia High School Graduation Tests
Hawaii	Stanford Achievement Test	Credit by Examination	Hawaii State Test of Essential Competencies
Idaho	Iowa Tests of Basic Skills/ Tests of Achievement and Proficiency	Direct Writing/Mathematics Assessment, Idaho Reading Indicator	
Illinois		Illinois Standards Achievement Tests	Prairie State Achievement Examination
Indiana		Indiana Statewide Testing for Educational Progress	
Iowa	(None)		
Kansas		(State-Developed Tests)	
Kentucky	Comprehensive Test of Basic Skills	Kentucky Core Content Tests	
Louisiana	Iowa Tests of Basic Skills	Louisiana Educational Assessment Program	Graduate Exit Exam
Maine		Maine Educational Assessment	High School Assessment Test
Maryland		Maryland School Performance Assessment Program, Maryland Functional Testing Program	

STATE	NORM-REFERENCED TEST	CRITERION-REFERENCED TEST	EXIT EXAM
Massachusetts		Massachusetts Comprehensive Assessment System	
Michigan		Michigan Educational Assessment Program	High School Test
Minnesota		Basic Standards Test	Profile of Learning
Mississippi	Comprehensive Test of Basic Skills	Subject Area Testing Program	Functional Literacy Examination
Missouri		Missouri Mastery and Achievement Test	
Montana	Iowa Tests of Basic Skills		
Nebraska			
Nevada	TerraNova		Nevada High School Proficiency Examination
New Hampshire		NH Educational Improvement and Assessment Program	
New Jersey		Elementary School Proficiency Test/Early Warning Test	High School Proficiency Test
New Mexico	TerraNova		New Mexico High School Competency Exam
New York		Pupil Evaluation Program/ Preliminary Competency Tests	Regents Competency Tests
North Carolina	Iowa Tests of Basic Skills	NC End of Grade Test	
North Dakota	TerraNova	ND Reading, Writing, Speaking, Listening, Math Test	
Ohio		Ohio Proficiency Tests	Ohio Proficiency Tests
Oklahoma	Iowa Tests of Basic Skills	Oklahoma Criterion- Referenced Tests	
Oregon		Oregon Statewide Assessment	
Pennsylvania		Pennsylvania System of School Assessment	
Rhode Island	Metropolitan Achievement Test	New Standards English Language Arts Reference Exam, New Standards Mathematics Reference Exam, Rhode Island Writing Assessment, and Rhode Island Health Education Assessment	
South Carolina	TerraNova	Palmetto Achievement Challenge Tests	High School Exit Exam
South Dakota	Stanford Achievement Test		
Tennessee	Tennessee Comprehensive Assessment Program	Tennessee Comprehensive Assessment Program	

STATE	NORM-REFERENCED TEST	CRITERION-REFERENCED TEST	EXIT EXAM
Texas		Texas Assessment of Academic Skills, End-of-Course Examinations	Texas Assessment of Academic Skills
Utah	Stanford Achievement Test	Core Curriculum Testing	
Vermont		New Standards Reference Exams	
Virginia	Stanford Achievement Test	Virginia Standards of Learning	Virginia Standards of Learning
Washington	Iowa Tests of Basic Skills	Washington Assessment of Student Learning	Washington Assessment of Student Learning
West Virginia	Stanford Achievement Test		
Wisconsin	TerraNova	Wisconsin Knowledge and Concepts Examinations	
Wyoming	TerraNova	Wyoming Comprehensive Assessment System	Wyoming Comprehensive Assessment System

Table 3 Standardized Test Schedules by State

STATE	KG	1	2	3	4	5	6	7	8	9	10	11	12	COMMENT
Alabama				X	X	X	X	X	X	X	X	X	X	
Alaska				X	X		X		X			X		
Arizona			X	X	X	X	X	X	X	X	X	X	X	
Arkansas					X	X		X	X		X	X	X	
California			X	X	X	X	X	X	X	X	X	X		
Colorado				X	X	X		X	X					
Connecticut					X		X		X					
Delaware				X	X	X			X		X	X		
District of Columbia		X	X	X	X	X	X	X	X	X	X	X		
Florida				X	X	X			X		X			There is no state-mandated norm-referenced testing. However, the state collects information furnished by local districts that elect to perform norm-referenced testing. The FCAT is administered to Grades 4, 8, and 10 to assess reading and Grades 5, 8, and 10 to assess math.
Georgia	X			X	X	X	X		X		X			
Hawaii				X			X		X		X			The Credit by Examination is voluntary and is given in Grade 8 in Algebra and Foreign Languages.
Idaho				X	X	X	X	X	X	X	X	X		
Illinois				X	X	X		X	X		X	X		Exit Exam failure will not disqualify students from graduation if all other requirements are met.
Indiana				X			X		X		X			
Iowa		*	*	*	*	*	*	*	*	*	*	*	*	*Iowa does not currently have a statewide testing program. Locally chosen assessments are administered to grades determined locally.
Kansas				X	X	X		X	X		X	X		

STATE	KG	1	2	3	4	5	6	7	8	9	10	11	12	COMMENT
Kentucky					X	X	X	X	X	X	X	X	X	
Louisiana				X	X	X	X	X	X	X	X	X	X	
Maine					X				X			X		
Maryland				X		X			X	X	X	X	X	
Massachusetts				X	X	X		X	X	X	X			
Michigan					X	X		X	X					
Minnesota				X		X			X	X	X	X	X	
Mississippi				X	X	X	X	X	X					Mississippi officials would not return phone calls or emails regarding this information.
Missouri			X	X	X	X	X	X	X	X	X			
Montana					X				X		X			The State Board of Education has decided to use a single norm-referenced test statewide beginning 2000–2001 school year.
Nebraska		**	**	**	**	**	**	**	**	**	**	**	**	**Decisions regarding testing are left to the individual school districts.
Nevada					X				X					Districts choose whether and how to test with norm-referenced tests.
New Hampshire				X			X				X			
New Jersey				X	X			X	X	X	X	X		
New Mexico					X		X		X					
New York				X	X	X	X	X	X	X			X	Assessment program is going through major revisions.
North Carolina	X			X	X	X	X		X	X			X	NRT Testing selects samples of students, not all.
North Dakota					X		X		X		X			
Ohio					X		X			X			X	
Oklahoma				X		X		X	X			X		
Oregon				X		X			X		X			

STATE	KG	1	2	3	4	5	6	7	8	9	10	11	12	COMMENT
Pennsylvania						X	X		X	X		X		
Rhode Island				X	X	X		X	X	X	X	X		
South Carolina				X	X	X	X	X	X	X	X	***	***	***Students who fail the High School Exit Exam have opportunities to take the exam again in grades 11 and 12.
South Dakota			X		X	X			X	X		X		
Tennessee			X	X	X	X	X	X	X					
Texas				X	X	X	X	X	X		X	X	X	
Utah		X	X	X	X	X	X	X	X	X	X	X	X	
Vermont					X	X	X		X	X	X	X		Rated by the Centers for Fair and Open Testing as a nearly model system for assessment.
Virginia				X	X	X	X		X	X		X		
Washington						X			X			X		
West Virginia				X	X	X	X	X	X	X	X	X		
Wisconsin						X				X		X		
Wyoming						X				X			X	

Testing Accommodations

The more testing procedures vary from one classroom or school to the next, the less we can compare the scores from one group to another. Consider a test in which the publisher recommends that three sections of the test be given in one 45-minute session per day on three consecutive days. School A follows those directions. To save time, School B gives all three sections of the test in one session lasting slightly more than two hours. We can't say that both schools followed the same testing procedures. Remember that the test publishers provide testing procedures so schools can administer the tests in as close a manner as possible to the way the tests were administered to the groups used to obtain test norms. When we compare students' scores to norms, we want to compare apples to apples, not apples to oranges.

Most schools justifiably resist making any changes in testing procedures. Informally, a teacher can make minor changes that don't alter the testing procedures, such as separating two students who talk with each other instead of paying attention to the test; letting Lisa, who is getting over an ear infection, sit closer to the front so she can hear better; or moving Jeffrey away from the window to prevent his looking out the window and daydreaming.

There are two groups of students who require more formal testing accommodations. One group of students is identified as having a disability under Section 504 of the Rehabilitation Act of 1973 (Public Law 93-112). These students face some challenge but, with reasonable and appropriate accommodation, can take advantage of the same educational opportunities as other students. That is, they have a condition that requires some accommodation for them.

Just as schools must remove physical barriers to accommodate students with disabilities, they must make appropriate accommodations to remove other types of barriers to students' access to education. Marie is profoundly deaf, even with strong hearing aids. She does well in school with the aid of an interpreter, who signs her teacher's instructions to her and tells her teacher what Marie says in reply. An appropriate accommodation for Marie would be to provide the interpreter to sign test instructions to her, or to allow her to watch a videotape with an interpreter signing test instructions. Such a reasonable accommodation would not deviate from standard testing procedures and, in fact, would ensure that Marie received the same instructions as the other students.

If your child is considered disabled and has what is generally called a Section 504 Plan or individual accommodation plan (IAP), then the appropriate way to ask for testing accommodations is to ask for them in a meeting to discuss school accommodations under the plan. If your child is not already covered by such a plan, he or she won't qualify for one merely because you request testing accommodations.

The other group of students who may receive formal testing accommodations are those identified as handicapped under the Individuals with Disabilities Education Act (IDEA)—students with mental retardation, learning disabilities, serious emotional disturbance, orthopedic handicap, hearing or visual problems, and other handicaps defined in the law. These students have been identified under procedures governed by federal and sometimes state law, and their education is governed by a document called the Individualized Educational Program (IEP). Unless you are under a court order specifically revoking your educational rights on behalf of your child, you are a full member of the IEP team even if you and your child's other parent are divorced and the other parent has custody. Until recently, IEP teams actually had the prerogative to exclude certain handicapped students from taking standardized group testing altogether. However, today states make it more difficult to exclude students from testing.

If your child is classified as handicapped and has an IEP, the appropriate place to ask for testing accommodations is in an IEP team meeting. In fact, federal regulations require IEP teams to address testing accommodations. You have the right to call a meeting at any time. In that meeting, you will have the opportunity to present your case for the accommodations you believe are necessary. Be prepared for the other team members to resist making extreme accommodations unless you can present a very strong case. If your child is identified as handicapped and you believe that he or she should be provided special testing accommodations, contact the person at your child's school who is responsible for convening IEP meetings and request a meeting to discuss testing accommodations.

Problems arise when a request is made for accommodations that cause major departures from standard testing procedures. For example, Lynn has an identified learning disability in mathematics calculation and attends resource classes for math. Her disability is so severe that her IEP calls for her to use a calculator when performing all math problems. She fully under-

stands math concepts, but she simply can't perform the calculations without the aid of a calculator. Now it's time for Lynn to take the school-based standardized tests, and she asks to use a calculator. In this case, since her IEP already requires her to be provided with a calculator when performing math calculations, she may be allowed a calculator during school standardized tests. However, because using a calculator constitutes a major violation of standard testing procedures, her score on all sections in which she is allowed to use a calculator will be recorded as a failure, and her results in some states will be removed from among those of other students in her school in calculating school results.

How do we determine whether a student is allowed formal accommodations in standardized school testing and what these accommodations may be? First, if your child is not already identified as either handicapped or disabled, having the child classified in either group solely to receive testing accommodations will be considered a violation of the laws governing both classifications. Second, even if your child is already classified in either group, your state's department of public instruction will provide strict guidelines for the testing accommodations schools may make. Third, even if your child is classified in either group and you are proposing testing accommodations allowed under state testing guidelines, any accommodations must still be both *reasonable* and *appropriate*. To be reasonable and appropriate, testing accommodations must relate to your child's disability and must be similar to those already in place in his or her daily educational program. If your child is always tested individually in a separate room for all tests in all subjects, then a similar practice in taking school-based standardized tests may be appropriate. But if your child has a learning disability only in mathematics calculation, requesting that all test questions be read to him or her is inappropriate because that accommodation does not relate to his identified handicap.

Glossary

Accountability The idea that a school district is held responsible for the achievement of its students. The term may also be applied to holding students responsible for a certain level of achievement in order to be promoted or to graduate.

Achievement test An assessment that measures current knowledge in one or more of the areas taught in most schools, such as reading, math, and language arts.

Aptitude test An assessment designed to predict a student's potential for learning knowledge or skills.

Content validity The extent to which a test represents the content it is designed to cover.

Criterion-referenced test A test that rates how thoroughly a student has mastered a specific skill or area of knowledge. Typically, a criterion-referenced test is subjective, and relies on someone to observe and rate student work; it doesn't allow for easy comparisons of achievement among students. Performance assessments are criterion-referenced tests. The opposite of a criterion-referenced test is a norm-referenced test.

Frequency distribution A tabulation of individual scores (or groups of scores) that shows the number of persons who obtained each score.

Generalizability The idea that the score on a test reflects what a child knows about a subject, or how well he performs the skills the test is supposed to be assessing. Generalizability requires that enough test items are administered to truly assess a student's achievement.

Grade equivalent A score on a scale developed to indicate the school grade (usually measured in months of a year) that corresponds to an average chronological age, mental age, test score, or other characteristic. A grade equivalent of 6.4 is interpreted as a score that is average for a group in the fourth month of Grade 6.

High-stakes assessment A type of standardized test that has major consequences for a student or school (such as whether a child graduates from high school or gets admitted to college).

Mean Average score of a group of scores.

Median The middle score in a set of scores ranked from smallest to largest.

National percentile Percentile score derived from the performance of a group of individuals across the nation.

Normative sample A comparison group consisting of individuals who have taken a test under standard conditions.

Norm-referenced test A standardized test that can compare scores of students in one school with a reference group (usually other students in the same grade and age, called the "norm group"). Norm-referenced tests compare the achievement of one student or the students of a school, school district, or state with the norm score.

Norms A summary of the performance of a group of individuals on which a test was standardized.

Percentile An incorrect form of the word *centile,* which is the percent of a group of scores that falls below a given score. Although the correct term is *centile,* much of the testing literature has adopted the term *percentile.*

Performance standards A level of performance on a test set by education experts.

Quartiles Points that divide the frequency distribution of scores into equal fourths.

Regression to the mean The tendency of scores in a group of scores to vary in the direction of the mean. For example: If a child has an abnormally low score on a test, she is likely to make a higher score (that is, one closer to the mean) the next time she takes the test.

Reliability The consistency with which a test measures some trait or characteristic. A measure can be reliable without being valid, but it can't be valid without being reliable.

Standard deviation A statistical measure used to describe the extent to which scores vary in a group of scores. Approximately 68 percent of scores in a group are expected to be in a range from one standard deviation below the mean to one standard deviation above the mean.

Standardized test A test that contains well-defined questions of proven validity and that produces reliable scores. Such tests are commonly paper-and-pencil exams containing multiple-choice items, true or false questions, matching exercises, or short fill-in-the-blanks items. These tests may also include performance assessment items (such as a writing sample), but assessment items cannot be completed quickly or scored reliably.

Test anxiety Anxiety that occurs in test-taking situations. Test anxiety can seriously impair individuals' ability to obtain accurate scores on a test.

Validity The extent to which a test measures the trait or characteristic it is designed to measure. Also see *reliability.*

Answer Keys for Practice Skills

Chapter 2:
Word Analysis

1 A
2 C
3 C
4 C
5 C
6 D

Chapter 3:
Vocabulary

1 C
2 C
3 A
4 D
5 D
6 A
7 C
8 B
9 A

Chapter 4:
Synonyms,
Antonyms,
and Homophones

1 B
2 C
3 B
4 B

5 D
6 B
7 D
8 A
9 C
10 B
11 B
12 B
13 B
14 D
15 A
16 C
17 A
18 B

Chapter 5:
Word Meanings
in Context

1 A
2 B
3 C
4 D
5 B
6 A
7 C
8 B
9 C
10 A
11 D

12 B
13 C

Chapter 6:
Word Sounds

1 A
2 C
3 D
4 A
5 A
6 B
7 B
8 C
9 A
10 B
11 C
12 C
13 C
14 B

Chapter 7:
Spelling

1 C
2 A
3 C
4 B
5 C
6 B

7 D
8 B
9 D
10 D
11 A

Chapter 8:
Language
Mechanics

1 A
2 D
3 B
4 B
5 A
6 C
7 C
8 B
9 C
10 B
11 A
12 B
13 B
14 A
15 C

Chapter 9:
Reading
Comprehension

1	B
2	D
3	B
4	D
5	D
6	B
7	C
8	B
9	C
10	C
11	D

Sample Practice Test

You may be riding a roller coaster of feelings and opinions at this point. If your child has gone through the preceding chapters easily, then you're both probably excited to move on, to jump in with both feet, take the test, and that will be that. On the other hand, your child may have struggled a bit with some of the chapters. Some of the concepts may be difficult for him and will require a little more practice. Never fear!

All children acquire skills in all areas of learning when they are developmentally ready. We can't push them, but we can reinforce the skills that they already know. In addition, we can play games and do activities to pave the way for their understanding of the skills that they will need to master later. With luck, that's what you've done with the preceding chapters.

The test that follows is designed to incorporate components of several different kinds of standardized tests. The test that your child takes in school probably won't look just like this one, but it should be sufficiently similar that he should be pretty comfortable with the format. The administration of tests varies as well. It is important that your child hear the rhythm and language used in standardized tests. If you wish, you may have your child read the directions that precede each test section to you first and explain what the item is asking

him to do. Your child may try it on his own if you feel he understands it, or you may want to clarify the instructions.

Test Administration

If you like, you may complete the entire test in one day, but it is not recommended that your child attempt to finish it in one sitting. As test administrator, you'll find that you'll need to stretch, have a snack, or use the bathroom too! If you plan to do the test in one day, leave at least 15 minutes between sessions.

Before you start, prepare a quiet place, free of distractions. Have two or three sharpened pencils with erasers that don't smudge and a flat, clear work space. As your child proceeds from item to item, encourage him to ask you if he doesn't understand something. In a real testing situation, questions are accepted, but the extent to which items can be explained is limited. Don't go overboard in making sure your child understands what to do. Your child will have to learn to trust his instincts somewhat.

The test shouldn't take all day. If your youngster seems to be dawdling along, enforce time limits and help him to understand that the real test will have time limits as well. Relax, and try to have fun!

To the Student:

These tests will give you a chance to put the tips you have learned to work.
A few last reminders . . .

- Be sure you understand all the directions before you begin each test. You may ask the teacher questions about the directions if you do not understand them.

- Work as quickly as you can during each test.

- When you change an answer, be sure to erase your first mark completely.

- You can guess at an answer or skip difficult items and go back to them later.

- Use the tips you have learned whenever you can.

- It is OK to be a little nervous. You may even do better.

Now that you have completed the lessons in this book, you are on your way to scoring high!

STUDENT'S NAME		SCHOOL
LAST	FIRST	MI	TEACHER

FEMALE ○   MALE ○

BIRTHDATE

MONTH	DAY		YEAR
JAN ○	⓪	⓪		⓪
FEB ○	①	①		①
MAR ○	②	②		②
APR ○	③	③		③
MAY ○		④		④
JUN ○		⑤	⑤	⑤
JUL ○		⑥	⑥	⑥
AUG ○		⑦	⑦	⑦
SEP ○		⑧	⑧	⑧
OCT ○		⑨	⑨	⑨
NOV ○				
DEC ○				

GRADE

① ② ③ ④ ⑤ ⑥

(Answer grid columns A–Z repeated for each letter of the student's name)

Word Analysis

1 ⒶⒷⒸⒹ	3 ⒶⒷⒸⒹ	5 ⒶⒷⒸⒹ	7 ⒶⒷⒸⒹ	9 ⒶⒷⒸⒹ
2 ⒶⒷⒸⒹ	4 ⒶⒷⒸⒹ	6 ⒶⒷⒸⒹ	8 ⒶⒷⒸⒹ	10 ⒶⒷⒸⒹ

Vocabulary

1 ⒶⒷⒸⒹ	3 ⒶⒷⒸⒹ	5 ⒶⒷⒸⒹ	7 ⒶⒷⒸⒹ	9 ⒶⒷⒸⒹ
2 ⒶⒷⒸⒹ	4 ⒶⒷⒸⒹ	6 ⒶⒷⒸⒹ	8 ⒶⒷⒸⒹ	10 ⒶⒷⒸⒹ

Synonyms, Antonyms, and Homophones

1 ⒶⒷⒸⒹ	5 ⒶⒷⒸⒹ	9 ⒶⒷⒸⒹ	12 ⒶⒷⒸⒹ	15 ⒶⒷⒸⒹ
2 ⒶⒷⒸⒹ	6 ⒶⒷⒸⒹ	10 ⒶⒷⒸⒹ	13 ⒶⒷⒸⒹ	16 ⒶⒷⒸⒹ
3 ⒶⒷⒸⒹ	7 ⒶⒷⒸⒹ	11 ⒶⒷⒸⒹ	14 ⒶⒷⒸⒹ	17 ⒶⒷⒸⒹ
4 ⒶⒷⒸⒹ	8 ⒶⒷⒸⒹ			

Word Meanings in Context

1 ⒶⒷⒸⒹ	4 ⒶⒷⒸⒹ	7 ⒶⒷⒸⒹ	9 ⒶⒷⒸⒹ	11 ⒶⒷⒸⒹ
2 ⒶⒷⒸⒹ	5 ⒶⒷⒸⒹ	8 ⒶⒷⒸⒹ	10 ⒶⒷⒸⒹ	12 ⒶⒷⒸⒹ
3 ⒶⒷⒸⒹ	6 ⒶⒷⒸⒹ			

Word Sounds

1 ⒶⒷⒸⒹ	4 ⒶⒷⒸⒹ	7 ⒶⒷⒸⒹ	10 ⒶⒷⒸⒹ	13 ⒶⒷⒸⒹ
2 ⒶⒷⒸⒹ	5 ⒶⒷⒸⒹ	8 ⒶⒷⒸⒹ	11 ⒶⒷⒸⒹ	14 ⒶⒷⒸⒹ
3 ⒶⒷⒸⒹ	6 ⒶⒷⒸⒹ	9 ⒶⒷⒸⒹ	12 ⒶⒷⒸⒹ	15 ⒶⒷⒸⒹ

Spelling

1 ⒶⒷⒸⒹ	4 ⒶⒷⒸⒹ	7 ⒶⒷⒸⒹ	9 ⒶⒷⒸⒹ	11 ⒶⒷⒸⒹ
2 ⒶⒷⒸⒹ	5 ⒶⒷⒸⒹ	8 ⒶⒷⒸⒹ	10 ⒶⒷⒸⒹ	12 ⒶⒷⒸⒹ
3 ⒶⒷⒸⒹ	6 ⒶⒷⒸⒹ			

Language Mechanics

1 ⒶⒷⒸⒹ	5 ⒶⒷⒸⒹ	9 ⒶⒷⒸⒹ	12 ⒶⒷⒸⒹ	15 ⒶⒷⒸⒹ
2 ⒶⒷⒸⒹ	6 ⒶⒷⒸⒹ	10 ⒶⒷⒸⒹ	13 ⒶⒷⒸⒹ	16 ⒶⒷⒸⒹ
3 ⒶⒷⒸⒹ	7 ⒶⒷⒸⒹ	11 ⒶⒷⒸⒹ	14 ⒶⒷⒸⒹ	17 ⒶⒷⒸⒹ
4 ⒶⒷⒸⒹ	8 ⒶⒷⒸⒹ			

Reading Comprehension

1 ⒶⒷⒸⒹ	4 ⒶⒷⒸⒹ	6 ⒶⒷⒸⒹ	8 ⒶⒷⒸⒹ	10 ⒶⒷⒸⒹ
2 ⒶⒷⒸⒹ	5 ⒶⒷⒸⒹ	7 ⒶⒷⒸⒹ	9 ⒶⒷⒸⒹ	11 ⒶⒷⒸⒹ
3 ⒶⒷⒸⒹ				

WORD ANALYSIS

Directions: Choose the correct answer for each of the following questions.

Example:

This is a picture of a ____at. What is the **first** letter?

  A   t

  B   s

  C   k

  D   c

Answer:

  D   c

☆

1   This is a picture of a _tar. What is the **first** letter?

  A   m

  B   h

  C   o

  D   s

2   This is a picture of a _ed. What is the **first** letter?

  A   p

  B   g

  C   b

  D   y

3   This is a picture of a _ree. What is the **first** letter?

  A   p

  B   h

  C   t

  D   l

GO →

4 This is a picture of a _at. What is the **first** letter?

A h

B r

C g

D d

5 This is a picture of a do_. What is the **last** letter?

A g

B b

C t

D h

6 Here is a picture of a ra_. What is the **last** letter?

A d

B t

C h

D k

7 Here is part of the alphabet: B C D _ F G H I J. Which letter is missing?

A B

B E

C G

D C

8 Which of these pairs of letters shows **different** letters?

A b B

B c C

C g G

D p Q

GO

9 Which of these pairs of letters shows the **same** letters?

   A q P

   B p Q

   C d B

   D f F

10 A _irl wears a dress. What is the **first** letter?

   A q

   B g

   C p

   D s

VOCABULARY

Directions: Choose the correct word to go in the blank in each of these sentences.

Example:

The cat ran up a _____.

A tree

B car

C hole

D grass

Answer:

A tree

1 Mother went to the _____ to buy some food.

A road

B office

C store

D school

2 Wayne could not _____ the teacher.

A hear

B eat

C sleep

D lose

3 We get milk from a _____.

A cat

B day

C cow

D chair

4 We ride to the city on a _____.

A dog

B bed

C bus

D bug

GO →

Directions: Look at each picture and choose the correct answer to each question.

Example:

Which of these words tells what the boy is doing?

A sleeping

B fishing

C running

D jumping

Answer:

A sleeping

5 Which of these words tells what the girl is doing?

A crying

B fishing

C sleeping

D eating

6 Which of these words tells what the children are doing?

A playing

B fighting

C crying

D singing

7 Which of these words tells what the horse is doing?

A sleeping

B barking

C jumping

D running

8 Where is Spot the cat hiding?

   A in the tree

   B in the dog house

   C in the bedroom

   D in the attic

Directions: Choose the correct picture to answer the question.

9 Which picture shows the children jumping rope?

A

B

C

D

10 Which picture shows the boy reading?

A

B

C

D

STOP

SYNONYMS, ANTONYMS, AND HOMOPHONES

Directions: Look at the underlined word in each sentence. Which word is a **synonym** (a word that means the same thing) for the underlined word?

Example:

I'm <u>glad</u> that I won the prize.

A happy

B afraid

C sorry

D mad

Answer:

A happy

1 My mom was <u>mad</u> when she lost her ring.

A happy

B angry

C sad

D good

2 Sam <u>hopped</u> across the lawn.

A jumped

B jogged

C ran

D walked

3 Ravi's brother <u>tripped</u> over the rock.

A fell

B hopped

C ran

D walked

4 That cat is really <u>pretty</u>.

A ugly

B plain

C beautiful

D old

Directions: Choose the pair in which the words mean the same thing.

Example:

A walk   run

B sleep   nap

C dog   horse

D go   stop

Answer:

B sleep   nap

GO

Cut along dashed line.

5 A blue   purple

  B fast   quick

  C mean   nice

  D run   walk

6 A pears   apples

  B drink   sip

  C slow   fast

  D fall   hop

7 A tiny   little

  B orange   pineapple

  C sit   stand

  D read   write

Directions: Look at each sentence and pick the word that means the **opposite** of the word that is underlined.

Example:

Keiko got to school quickly. She is going to be <u>early</u>.

  A mad

  B glad

  C late

  D sick

Answer:

  C late

8 Jose was <u>dirty</u> after playing football.

  A clean

  B late

  C ill

  D cold

9 I <u>walked</u> down the hall.

  A sold

  B got

  C ate

  D ran

10 At dawn it gets <u>light</u>.

  A thick

  B black

  C dark

  D late

Directions: Choose the pair in which the words are opposite in meaning.

Example:

  A dry   wet

  B slow   long

  C green   white

  D push   eat

Answer:

  A dry   wet

GO

11 A ears   mouth
   B clean   dirty
   C in   down
   D house   town

12 A hard   soft
   B up   high
   C hop   jump
   D cat   kitten

13 A fast   duck
   B bad   gold
   C rich   poor
   D big   huge

Directions: Choose the pair of words that are homophones.

Example:

   A pear   pair
   B read   right
   C blue   red
   D boy   girl

Answer:

   A pear   pair

14 A hot   heat
   B not   knot
   C bat   hat
   D bird   dog

15 A on   one
   B for   four
   C boy   by
   D up   down

Directions: Which homophone correctly fits in the sentence.

Example:

My team _____ our game.

   A got
   B ball
   C one
   D won

Answer:

   D won

16 The fish swim in the _____.

   A sky
   B tree
   C see
   D sea

17 I will _____ you a present.

   A by
   B bye
   C buy
   D bear

STOP

WORD MEANINGS IN CONTEXT

Directions: Read each sentence and choose the word that best fits in the blank.

Example:

It was time to go to _____, so Sarah put on her nightgown.

A sink

B bed

C tub

D book

Answer:

B bed

1 The _____ child was able to break the piñata.

A oldest

B strongest

C youngest

D prettiest

2 Jane was so _____ she could touch the fan on the ceiling.

A tall

B short

C good

D bad

3 Kim Sun could not eat the candy apple because it was too _____ to chew.

A slow

B sweet

C hard

D fast

4 Her sister crawled away because Sue forgot to _____ the door.

A push

B swing

C open

D close

5 Latoya was too _____ to drive a car.

A old

B young

C rich

D mean

6 Jim was _____ of the growling tiger.

A scared

B happy

C mad

D wild

GO

Cut along dashed line

7 Ammon was _____. He had a fever.

   A hungry

   B good

   C sick

   D sad

8 He was _____ because his friend took his glove.

   A slow

   B quick

   C angry

   D come

Directions: Read the paragraph below. Find the word below the paragraph that best fits in each numbered blank.

Example:

Jake got a new __1__ for her birthday. He liked to chew __2__.

  1 **A** puppy   **2** **A** games

     B fun   **B** shoes

     C dolphins   **C** friend

     D toy   **D** birthday

Answers:

  1 **A** puppy   **2** **B** shoes

Cassie and Elizabeth went to a horse show. They watched horses jump over __9__. For lunch they bought a sandwich and a cool __10__. The __11__ felt warm on their skin. By the end of the long, busy day, they were tired but __12__.

  9 **A** mud

     B fences

     C balls

     D coats

 10 **A** prize

     B rock

     C drink

     D oven

 11 **A** oven

     B moon

     C flies

     D sunshine

 12 **A** sad

     B angry

     C happy

     D green

WORD SOUNDS

Directions: Read each question and choose the correct answer.

Example:

In which pair do the words **begin** with the same sound?

A bat   pig

B city   cool

C can   kid

D go   jump

Answer:

C can   kid

---

1 In which pair do the words **begin** with the same sound?

A hen   when

B ball   pen

C hair   hat

D can   chin

---

2 In which pair do the words **begin** with the same sound?

A fun   get

B shine   jump

C goat   get

D dog   cat

---

3 In which pair do the words **begin** with the same sound?

A queen   quote

B oven   ice

C gas   jelly

D ran   pig

---

4 <u>G</u> is for <u>get</u>. <u>H</u> is for <u>hat</u>. <u>J</u> is for <u>jelly</u>. What is <u>K</u> for?

A church

B chain

C chin

D kind

---

5 Choose the word that begins with the same sound as the word <u>bird</u>.

A bunny

B seat

C lamb

D glass

GO →

Directions: Choose the correct answer for each of the following questions.

Example:

Which of these words has the same **ending** sound as in the word <u>cart</u>?

A sag

B sat

C sip

D case

Answer:

B sat

---

6 Choose the words with the same **ending** sound.

A tart   feet

B sun   basket

C big   truck

D show   hard

---

7 Which of these words has a different **ending** sound than the others?

A rag

B rug

C rip

D rig

8 Which word has the same **ending** sound as the word for this picture?

A witch

B wash

C crack

D church

Directions: Choose the letter that makes the **ending** sound as in the word for the picture below.

Example:

A S

B P

C H

D R

Answer:

D R

9 Choose the letter that makes the **ending** sound as in the word for the picture below.

    A D

    B T

    C G

    D S

Directions: Match the word with the same **vowel** sound as the underlined word in each question.

Example:

Which word has the same **vowel** sound as in <u>loot</u>?

    A loop

    B hop

    C nap

    D hip

Answer:

    A loop

10 Which word has the same **vowel** sound as in <u>neat</u>?

    A sweet

    B red

    C said

    D bed

11 Which word has the same **vowel** sound as in <u>broke</u>?

    A head

    B road

    C cat

    D cool

12 Which word has the same **vowel** sound as in <u>sign</u>?

    A sun

    B sat

    C mile

    D moon

GO

Directions: Choose the correct answer for each of the following questions.

Example:

Which of these animal names rhymes with <u>cat</u>?

A hippo

B bear

C rat

D hare

Answer:

C rat

---

13 Which of these words rhymes with <u>bread</u>?

A bad

B rid

C bed

D rod

14 Which of these words rhymes with <u>nest</u>?

A beat

B nut

C barn

D best

---

15 Which two words rhyme?

A all, air

B hog, slog

C ran, run

D get, gull

Cut along dashed line.

SPELLING

Directions: Choose the **correctly** spelled word in each question.

Example:

   A note

   B noat

   C noit

   D nout

Answer:

   A note

---

1 A cake

   B caik

   C cak

   D kake

---

2 A hors

   B hurse

   C horse

   D hoars

---

3 A smil

   B smail

   C smile

   D smal

Directions: Choose the answer to fill in the blank correctly.

4 Pat and Sandy are friends. Pat is short and Sandy is ta__. What letters go in the blank?

   A tt

   B dd

   C ll

   D ss

5 The __ook is filled with fish.

   A ch

   B br

   C bo

   D bl

GO ⇨

6 The man is wearing a _at.

A c

B h

C i

D r

Directions: Choose the word that is spelled **correctly.**

7 A tran

B traine

C train

D trin

8 A bear

B bir

C beare

D bur

9 A flur

B flower

C flor

D fleure

10 A orang

B oringe

C orange

D orang

Directions: Choose the word that is spelled **incorrectly.**

11 A heart

B cart

C church

D wher

12 A barn

B goat

C goos

D girl

LANGUAGE MECHANICS

Directions: Read these sentences. Then choose the word that should begin with a capital letter.

Example:

Our friends are moving to ohio.

A friends

B are

C moving

D ohio

Answer:

D ohio

1 We are going to disneyland for our summer vacation.

A going

B disneyland

C summer

D vacation

2 Sue went to the park on tuesday night.

A went

B park

C tuesday

D night

3 jim rode his scooter down the street.

A jim

B rode

C scooter

D street

4 ginger pye the cat likes to play ball.

A ginger pye

B cat

C likes

D ball

Directions: Choose the sentence that shows **correct** capitalization.

Example:

A Tim is Going to town today.

B I love Chocolate pudding.

C In March, we go to Paris.

D where are you going?

Answer:

C In March, we go to Paris.

GO

Cut along dashed line.

5 A tomico and Sam are making snowballs.

B I like to ride the subway when I go to New York City.

C Jamie has a birthday on tuesday, March 16.

D The Peach pie was good, but the Apple pie was the best!

---

6 A Jorge took his dog to Town.

B I want to go home.

C My birthday is in april.

D what day is it?

---

7 A Let's go to the Park.

B Tom and emma went to buy pizza.

C Today is Monday, September 7.

D My rabbit's name is john.

Directions: Read each sentence and choose the correct answer.

Example:

Which sentence is punctuated correctly?

A Brent rode his. bike to town.

B Brent. rode his bike to town.

C Brent rode his bike to town.

D Brent rode his bike to. town.

Answer:

C Brent rode his bike to town.

---

8 Which sentence is punctuated correctly?

A Will here is your book?

B Will. Here is your book.

C Will, here is your book.

D Will here is your book

---

9 Which sentence is punctuated correctly?

A Crystal, that's a nice project!

B Crystal that's, a nice project!

C Crystal, that's, a nice project.

D Crystal, that's a nice, project.

---

10 Which of these sentences is punctuated correctly?

A Harold, please finish your cake?

B I don't think that the teacher is here.

C Watch out for that, fire.

D Where, are you going.

GO →

Directions: Read each sentence and choose the correct word to fill in the blank.

Example:

Shonda _____ going to win first place.

A are

B were

C be

D is

Answer:

D is

---

11 Herman and Shane _____ going to the store.

A are

B is

C would

D be

---

12 _____ you going to get a new haircut?

A Is

B Ain't

C Are

D Was

---

13 _____ you ever been to a play?

A Have

B Are

C Were

D Was

---

14 My sister is _____ than Rachel's sister.

A small

B smallest

C smaller

D smalls

---

15 Yesterday we saw one cat. Today we saw two _____.

A cat

B catz

C cats

D catten

GO

Directions: Read each sentence. Choose the correct pronoun for the underlined words.

Example:

Please take <u>Mary and me</u> to the park.

A us

B them

C they

D we

Answer:

A us

---

16 I like to play with <u>Ben</u>.

A her

B him

C us

D them

---

17 That sled belongs to <u>Jim and me</u>.

A them

B ours

C us

D we

Cut along dashed line.

STOP

READING COMPREHENSION

Directions: Parent says to child: "I am going to read you a part of the story. Then choose what you think might happen next."

Parent reads:

Four of Jimmy's friends came to the door. One had a glove. Another had a ball. Two had bats. They all went out to Jimmy's backyard.

1 What were the boys going to do?

   A play baseball

   B sing

   C build a fort

   D play soccer

Parent reads:

Kara got out a recipe book. Then she got out some milk, flour, and sugar. She mixed everything together. Next, she poured the batter into a pan. She put the pan in the oven. After a while, she took the pan out of the oven and placed it on the counter to cool. Soon it would be time to ice it and put in some candles. Then she would carry it out to her mother as a surprise.

2 What was Kara doing?

   A making mud pies

   B cleaning the kitchen

   C baking a cake

   D doing her homework

3 Why was Kara making a cake?

   A She was hungry.

   B It was her mother's birthday.

   C It was time for breakfast.

   D Her teacher was hungry.

Directions: Look at each picture and answer the question about it.

Example:

Why are these children happy?

   A They are eating dinner.

   B They are playing a game.

   C They are sleeping.

   D They are watching a movie.

Answer:

   B They are playing a game.

Cut along dashed line.

4 What do you think the people are watching?

A a movie

B a baseball game

C a car race

D a pet show

5 Why is this child sad?

A He is saying goodbye to someone.

B He lost his favorite toy.

C His brother teased him.

D He broke a lamp.

Directions: Read each sentence below. Decide which word goes with the sentence.

Example:

When you go to sleep, use one of these.

A pillow

B drink

C bandage

D pencil

Answer:

A pillow

6 If you want a drink, use this.

A cup

B dog

C bed

D car

7 If you see a sad movie, you might do this.

A cry

B laugh

C fall asleep

D run away

Directions: Read the story and then answer the questions.

My name is Frosty. I like to eat hay. My little girl brings me sugar lumps. I live in the barn with a cat and a goat. I like to jump over fences. I neigh when I am hungry.

8 What is Frosty?

A rabbit

B horse

C mouse

D chicken

9 What does Frosty like to eat?

A goats

B hay

C cheese

D milk

A new family moved in next door. They have a boy my age. He is a soccer star. Saturday the doorbell rang. My mom answered the door. She came into my room with a new boy. "This is David," she said. He was carrying a soccer ball.

10 Who is David?

A the boy's father

B the boy's uncle

C the new neighbor

D the boy's brother

11 What did David bring with him?

A a soccer ball

B a blanket

C a puppy

D a pizza

STOP

Answer Key
for Sample Practice Test

Word Analysis

1	D
2	C
3	C
4	A
5	A
6	B
7	B
8	D
9	D
10	B

Vocabulary

1	C
2	A
3	C
4	C
5	B
6	A
7	D
8	A
9	C
10	D

Synonyms, Antonyms, and Homophones

1	B
2	A
3	A
4	C

5	B
6	B
7	A
8	A
9	D
10	C
11	B
12	A
13	C
14	B
15	B
16	D
17	C

Word Meanings in Context

1	B
2	A
3	C
4	D
5	B
6	A
7	C
8	C
9	B
10	C
11	D
12	C

Word Sounds

1	C
2	C

3	A
4	D
5	A
6	A
7	C
8	B
9	C
10	A
11	B
12	C
13	C
14	D
15	B

Spelling

1	A
2	C
3	C
4	C
5	B
6	B
7	C
8	A
9	B
10	C
11	D
12	C

Language Mechanics

1	B
2	C

3	A
4	A
5	B
6	B
7	C
8	C
9	A
10	B
11	A
12	C
13	A
14	C
15	C
16	B
17	C

Reading Comprehension

1	A
2	C
3	B
4	C
5	A
6	A
7	A
8	B
9	B
10	C
11	A